Surge
of Piety

Surge of Piety

*Norman Vincent Peale
and the Remaking of
American Religious Life*

CHRISTOPHER LANE

Yale UNIVERSITY PRESS

New Haven and London

Yale University Press books may be purchased in quantity for educational, business, or promotional use. For information, please e-mail sales.press@yale.edu (U.S. office) or sales@yaleup.co.uk (U.K. office).

Set in Minion type by Integrated Publishing Solutions.
Printed in the United States of America.

Library of Congress Control Number: 2016937984
ISBN 978-0-300-20373-8 (hardcover : alk. paper)

A catalogue record for this book is available from the British Library.

This paper meets the requirements of ANSI/NISO Z39.48-1992 (Permanence of Paper).

10 9 8 7 6 5 4 3 2 1

Contents

Surge
of Piety

Introduction

In the winter of 1936, as political tensions pushed Europe once more to the brink of war, Norman Vincent Peale, the New York minister and soon-to-be best-selling author of *The Power of Positive Thinking*, gave one of his darkest political sermons. The "issue of the hour," he warned his congregation and the attendant press, was a fierce cultural battle between Christ and Marx. Although rising militarism in Germany and Japan would lead both countries to declare war on the United States five winters later, to Peale neither was an immediate threat. In the stark opposition he conjured, the nation faced a graver danger and an increasingly urgent imperative: it must "choose between Church and the Reds."[1]

Peale was not alone in using fear of communism to stoke religious sentiment across the United States. Throughout the 1930s and 1940s, as much of the world succumbed to totalitarianism, influential politicians and religious leaders in the United States pressed hard on the idea that in religion the nation would find both unity and redemption. Together, they cast the country as distinguished by its commitment to "Freedom Under God," to "Spiritual Mobilization," and to various "crusades," all of them aligning religious nationalism with spiritual uplift and resilience. Peale, by then one of the nation's most prominent and vocal ministers, played an outsize role in connecting that message to positive psychology and religiopsychiatry and to broadcasting their claims. Urging Americans to find a religious solution to their problems, he gave belief in oneself and country religious significance. To be a normal and healthy American, he asserted, was to be a devout one.

Peale's ultimatum—"choose between Church and the Reds"—persuaded Americans in large numbers to take refuge from communism in evangelical Christianity, including its re-

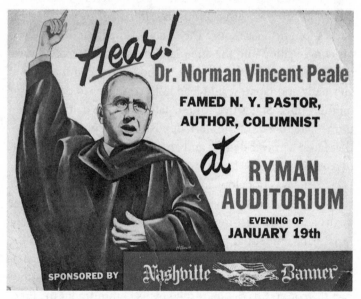

"Hear! Dr. Norman Vincent Peale, Famed N. Y. Pastor, Author, Columnist." Poster for talk at Ryman Auditorium, Nashville, January 19, 1951. Norman Vincent Peale Papers, Special Collections Research Center, Syracuse University Libraries.

"Dr. Peale Tells Thousands Here—The Future Belongs To Christ
Not Communism," *Nashville Banner,* January 20, 1951. Norman
Vincent Peale Papers, Special Collections Research Center,
Syracuse University Libraries.

ligiously themed perspective on physical and mental health.[2]
How he set about doing so is the subject of this book. We will
reach far into his personal and administrative papers and examine the organizations over which he presided and the close
alliances that he nurtured in the upper echelons of Washington, D.C. His friends and supporters ranged from conservative
pastors, corporate leaders, and federal agencies to the nation's
highly devout commander in chief, Dwight D. Eisenhower.
Peale's affinity with such natural allies helped to make anticommunism—and, subsequently, much of positive thinking
and significant currents in psychiatry—fervently pro-Christian.

Together these factors transformed the nation and its religious life. They reassigned health and well-being as categories "under God," and success as the consequence of strong religious conviction. All the while, and quite predictably, public religiosity rose to stratospheric levels.

The postwar borderland between religion and psychiatry turned out to be fertile ground for the evangelical nationalism that would revolutionize political conservatism across America. In view of Peale's extended involvement in such movements, his religious anticommunism and nationalism, though not exceptional, form an inescapable backdrop to his later emphasis on positive thinking and "practical" Christianity. For many years, his political sermons drew almost weekly newspaper headlines, such as "Clergyman Scores County Politicians for Their Betrayal of Religion."[3] Privately, Peale confided to close associates his core belief that "one of the best ways to undercut Communism [was] to reach the masses of the people with some simple religious principles."[4] These blended positive psychology with positive theology, popularizing a "gospel of reassurance and self-assurance" for an age of mass anxiety.[5]

There were, granted, ample grounds for concern. Given a decade-long slump blighting the U.S. economy, the war against the Axis powers of Japan-Germany-Italy, a grinding, unwinnable conflict in Korea, and a lengthy, dangerous nuclear standoff with the Soviet Union, insecurity was rampant. "These are ominous days . . . days of swift and shocking developments," President Franklin D. Roosevelt warned a joint session of Congress in May 1940, as Germany invaded the Low Countries and France, and Japan readied its air force to attack the U.S. fleet at Pearl Harbor. As the historian Ira Katznelson observes, "Fear about warfare and global violence became a permanent condition. It became an inextricable part of American consciousness."[6]

What was needed, Peale and others believed, were ways to bring "energy to despair," to restore a sense of security and unite the country in its beliefs.[7] In framing his message as one of essential faith in God, self, and country, the author of *The Power of Positive Thinking* assured the nation that it would not merely be "inoculated" against communism; it would be braced with "enthusiasm for Christian world conquest."[8]

As his press coverage shifted to column titles such as "Peale Fears 'Red' Aspect of Agitation Is a Token of Un-American Trends," Peale described the nation as undergoing "a second revolution," one treating the economic and broader cultural characteristics of the New Deal with almost religious respect.[9] "In the old days people flocked to church to pray to God that the evidences of His displeasure might pass," he opined. "Today they pray to the government to write another code."[10]

Peale, by then minister of New York's Marble Collegiate Church, was not alone in urging the use of religion in what has since been called a "public relations war against the New Deal."[11] In 1939, his longtime friend and supporter Howard W. Prentis, Jr., president of the National Association of Manufacturers, joined him in touting "a revival of American patriotism and religious faith" as the "only antidote" to the "virus of collectivism." According to Prentis, that "virus" included "the Naziism of New Liberalism."[12] "Every Christian should oppose the totalitarian trends of the New Deal," added the Reverend James W. Fifield, Jr., minister at the affluent First Congregational Church in Los Angeles and another old friend and supporter.[13] In December 1939, Fifield took out a full-page ad in the *Los Angeles Times* to denounce the New Deal while advertising the services of Spiritual Mobilization. The organization's central mission, he later explained, was "to arouse the ministers of all denominations in America to check the trends toward pagan stateism, which would destroy our basic freedom and spiritual ideals."[14] Over the next decade, with Peale's full support as a member of the advisory board, the organization would exert considerable influence on the way Americans understood themselves religiously.

Peale was without doubt one of the "conservative clergymen deployed ... to discredit Franklin D. Roosevelt's New Deal," notes the Princeton historian Kevin M. Kruse.[15] This role will be confirmed and amplified many times in this book as we follow the development of organizations with which Peale was closely associated—from the partisan, archconservative Committee for Constitutional Government to the American Foundation of Religion and Psychiatry (of which he was cofounder and long-term president). Opposition to the New Deal was also, initially, central to his message and fast-growing influence. Peale once called Roosevelt "a presumptuous seeker after improper power," concerning strife over appointees to the Supreme Court, and publicly rebuked the president for his "indifference to religion" when he skipped church to enjoy quiet fishing trips. In a preview of the McCarthy era and of Peale's role in its drumbeat against communism, one of his 1929 sermons was summed up as "Love of Deity Loyalty Test."[16]

Nor did the reverend's open "enthusiasm for Christian world conquest" lack an occasional threat to the unreligious or disbelieving. Almost a decade before his friend and admirer J. Edgar Hoover spoke of the need to "quarantine communism" because of the "diabolic machinations of sinister figures engaged in un-American activities," the minister from Ohio warned from his Manhattan pulpit in 1936, "The man who shows no interest in Christianity and fails to support it is the real enemy of our social institutions."[17]

"The real enemy." As Cold War tensions mounted in the 1950s and much of eastern Europe succumbed to Soviet occupation, pro-Christian anticommunism in the United States became a popular way of arousing religious sentiment nationally. Representative Louis C. Rabaut, a Democrat from suburban Detroit, summed up the picture in 1954 when telling other lawmakers in the House of Representatives, "You may argue from dawn to dusk about differing political, economic, and social systems, but the fundamental issue which is the unbridgeable gap between America and Communist Russia is a belief in Almighty God."[18] Religion filled the airwaves and saturated the nation's capital. "Almighty God," the new president Eisenhower prayed at his 1953 inauguration, "as we stand here at this moment my future associates in the Executive branch of the Government join me in beseeching that Thou will make full and complete our dedication to the service of the people in this throng and their fellow citizens everywhere."[19]

As Kruse has shown from a variety of angles and a trove of sources, the effort to represent the United States as "one nation under God" drew much of its impetus from religious-conservative reaction to the New Deal.[20] In 1951, Spiritual Mobilization—a group spearheaded by Fifield, Peale, and others—adjusted the focus from religious anticommunism to religious nationalism by announcing the formation of a new Committee to Proclaim Liberty. Broadcasting its desire to devote the festivities around Independence Day that year to the nation's "Freedom Under God," the committee placed ads nationwide, urging Americans to "declare that the rights God gave you may not be taken away by any government on any pretense."[21] Along with its highly successful "Perils to Freedom" competition of the previous decade, the committee was instrumental in encouraging Americans to think of their elected representatives as giving them nothing less than "government under God."

Blending sermon and political tract, Fifield had declared in a sermon, *The Cross vs. the Sickle,* that America should "quit temporizing" with the Soviet Union and "return to the Cross."[22] Not to be outdone by a vocal and increasingly influential Los Angeles neighbor, Hollywood came up with barely concealed propaganda in *The Sickle or the Cross* (1949). The film warned anxious Americans of the need to fight communism zealously and of the godlessness it represented at home and abroad.[23] The charismatic evangelist Billy Graham, later doyen to the Nixon White House, adopted the same line to cast small-town America as an idyllic place menaced by waves of advancing unbelief: "A great sinister anti-Christian movement masterminded by Satan has declared war upon the Christian God!"[24]

The message that the United States must choose between communism and religion—issuing from 1930s religious conservatives like Peale—was repeated so often that by midcentury it had cemented ties among patriotism, religiosity, and an evangelical understanding of mental health, with lasting implications for the country as a whole. Expressions of religious belief assumed signs of national unity and personal resilience. At the epicenter of such forces, President Eisenhower described religious faith as both the motivation that kept him going and his own personal shield against mental illness.[25]

The "shield" of religiosity turned out to have additional, political uses. A month before his inauguration, Eisenhower told the country, in a statement much repeated, "Our form of government has no sense unless it is founded in a deeply felt religious belief, and I don't care what it is."[26] The genial Ike evidently cared quite a lot; he had been swept into office after announcing at the Republican convention, "Ladies and gentlemen, you have summoned me to lead a great crusade." The last word was repeated three times in almost as many sentences.[27] The country had been "getting too secular," opined the president, who let himself appear in Peale's advertisements for *Guideposts* and *Spirit-Lifters,* the minister's blockbuster publications, as if the White House were personally endorsing them.[28]

After just one year in office, Eisenhower signed a bill to add the phrase "under God" to the Pledge of Allegiance, at a stroke transforming the very definition of the republic. In doing so, he told the country and the observing world, Americans would henceforth be daily proclaiming the "dedication of our nation and our people to the Almighty."[29] By 1955, when the nation's surge in religiosity was still three years from a postwar high, American dollars—on behalf of every citizen, devout or not—began to appear with the assurance, the insistence, "In God We Trust." An unmistakable religious message would thereafter accompany every cash transaction in U.S. currency, nationally and abroad.

Religious messages also came from quarters as diverse as the Pentagon and the Federal Bureau of Investigation, leading one commentator to remark on the astonishing rise in "piety along the Potomac."[30] During the Korean War, American servicemen were told repeatedly that theirs was a "covenant" or "redeemer" nation. In combat the United States would recognize its "dependence upon God" while acting as a "savior" to others.[31] "Since Communists are anti-God," Hoover warned parents, "encourage your child to be active in the church."[32] Peale would privately indicate that he admired Hoover's taking advantage of his position as director of the F.B.I. to make such statements.[33] The nation would be united and distinguished by its piety, which ministers such as Peale noted as a sign that its citizens were living as "God's own people." With Peale's involvement, an ecumenical Back to God crusade by the American Legion helped to solidify that thinking in fall 1951. A simple, highly effective message appeared in homes, schools, and places of worship nationwide: "Go to Church."

Unsurprisingly, attendance at churches and synagogues across America rose significantly—upward of 10 percent over the previous decade. By 1950, notes Kruse, "the percentage of Americans claiming a church membership climbed to 57 percent and then spiked to an all-time high of 69 percent at the end of the decade."[34] In a reversal of trends across northern Europe and Scandinavia, polls in the United States recorded a massive 95 percent of Americans claiming to be religious, with only 5 percent expressing "no preference."[35]

In the shadow of the hydrogen bomb and the frantic arms and space race that developed with the Soviet Union, "I've Got Religion," "The Teen Commandments," and "Big Fellow in the Sky" were hits on the radio and jukeboxes. The iconic Elvis Presley sang "I Believe" in 1957, offering listeners reassurance that "someone in the great somewhere / Hears . . . the smallest prayer." The postwar rush to the suburbs and the boom in car ownership led to a brief craze for drive-in churches. Newly designed dolls could be adjusted to praying positions. Keen to tap into the heightened religious enthusiasm, Hollywood brought out one spectacle after another. From Cecil B. DeMille's lavish *Ten Commandments* to William Wyler's panoramic *Ben-Hur: A Tale of the Christ,* each closely associated Christianity with political and spiritual emancipation.[36] "The great clash between two beliefs is dramatized," DeMille explained of his film, which would become one of the most commercially successful of all time.[37] Part of its legacy was a prominent nationwide campaign (led by the Eagles' Youth Guidance Commission) to establish monuments to the Ten Commandments on public property.[38]

"Religion is enjoying the biggest boom it has ever had in our country," Peale enthused in 1950, in a *Reader's Digest* article where he bluntly advised, "Let the Church Speak Up for Capitalism."[39] Well positioned to encourage the religious wave, and drawing on it eagerly to advance his own vision for America and self-fulfillment, Peale wrote *The Power of Positive Thinking*, which surged up the nonfiction best-seller list and stayed on it for 186 consecutive weeks, selling more copies in the United States in 1953 and 1954 than any fiction or nonfiction book except the Bible.[40] (It has since sold more than five million copies in fifteen languages and still sells more than twenty thousand copies a year.)[41] In the book, Peale made reference to God ninety-one times, with forty-nine further allusions to the Bible. Over and over he stressed, religious belief was a precondition for belief in oneself and the health that can accompany it.

With Peale's Manhattan church housing its own Religio-Psychiatric Clinic (funded by his book royalties, with additional support from Stanley Kresge, president of the S. S. Kresge retail organization), his influence soon extended far beyond the Christianity versus communism debate. Eventually it included, in ways frequently criticized, solutions for the nation's frosty relations among religion, psychiatry, and positive psychology. In Peale's hands, religio-psychiatry served aims similar to his religious conservatism and anticommunism: it urged Americans to find religious solutions to their problems. His pivot from politics to "practical" Christianity and spiritual-mental health stemmed from an argument that religious faith amounted to much more than a set of beliefs, practices, and traditions: it was also a force both personal and political. "We have made the mistake," he told his congregation and gathered reporters, of "thinking that Christianity is a creed to be recited. On the contrary, it is a power to be tapped."[42]

In encouraging that shift from creed to power, Peale teamed up with both religious conservatives and the psychiatrist Smiley Blanton. A devout Christian, Blanton had undergone brief training analysis with Sigmund Freud in Vienna shortly before Nazi persecution and anti-Semitism compelled Freud to seek sanctuary in London. During the sessions, as Blanton would describe in vivid detail in his memoir, he repeatedly quizzed Freud about the power of religious faith, or "transference," and how it might be harnessed for both personal gain and national transformation.

In New York City, excited about his recent European visit, Blanton joined Peale to found their clinic (1937) and the national organization that would later emerge out of it (1953). Under the banner "Toward Mental Health for All," the American Foundation of Religion and Psychiatry, Inc., promoted on a much larger scale the fusion of belief in self with belief in God.[43] Concerned about rising rates of anxiety and depression, the foundation called itself "an enterprise in the field of human betterment" and preached that "the lack of a religious outlook on life [was] at the heart of many emotional problems."[44] At peak influence in the late fifties, it promoted the idea that health was broadly synonymous with religious salvation. Peale, by then one of the nation's most visible and influential ministers, was with Blanton able to assert that religiosity epitomized robust American citizenship, an argument that persists in many parts of the country today.

How they succeeded and where they failed is the focus of

this book, as is the broader story of America's religious landscape and its complex, sometimes hostile relation to science. Drawing heavily on Blanton's sessions with Freud, the psychiatrist and the minister quickly redefined the unconscious in religious terms. They presented it to readers, listeners, and patients as a mostly untapped power that was benign and divine— not, as Freud had argued, presocial and aggressive. A deficit of religious belief ("estrangement from God") was said to trigger neurosis; revived religious faith was designated its cure.[45] In this respect, in a key sidebar to our story, Freud can be seen to have played an unexpected role in America's postwar religious revival, one that the self-described "heretic" and critic of religion could neither have wanted nor probably ever have imagined.[46]

Though little known today, the American Foundation of Religion and Psychiatry was by the late 1950s deemed one of the nation's "principal platforms for the encounter between religion and science."[47] Based largely on Peale's celebrity, its influence soon reached the White House, the F.B.I., and the nation's largest corporations, including its best-known carmakers and pharmaceutical companies.[48] It set up programs to influence political and religious leaders, encouraged ministers to ditch the "Social Gospel" of the New Deal for that of individualism and free enterprise, and sought ways to foster theological thinking across America, especially in the nation's pastoral care and definitions of mental health. The consequences of integrating religion and science into phenomena they interpret differently serve as a cautionary tale today.

The foundation researched, sponsored, and heavily promoted the concept of religio-psychiatry, which long predated Peale but shared with his outlook the determination that treatment for mental illness "must be religious as well as psychological."[49] Peale's phenomenal best-sellers, popular radio shows, and weekly television spots all emphasized that point of view. Patients were encouraged to accept "religiously motivated ideas and ideals as a means of solving personal problems."[50] Doctors were urged to make a clear and unmistakable "proclamation of faith."[51] As with Peale's religious anticommunism, Americans as a whole were urged to see religion as essential to their health and harmony. In *Surge of Piety* we revisit how a sizable portion of the country came to believe in that doctrine.

Peale grew up in Bowersville, Ohio, the son of a Methodist pastor who was a strong advocate for the temperance movement. As a boy, he helped his family by selling pots and pans door-to-door. In 1922, after studying at Ohio Wesleyan University and then at Boston University's School of Theology, he was ordained a Methodist minister, and for the next decade he pastored churches in Rhode Island and in Brooklyn and Syracuse, New York. Having previously suffered, in his words, "the worst inferiority complex of all," he devised a method of positive thinking that combined ardent self-belief with what he called "applied Christianity: a simple yet scientific system of practical techniques of successful living."[52]

Blanton, a devout Freudian psychiatrist from Unionville, Tennessee, studied medicine at Cornell and psychiatry at Johns Hopkins before embarking on a restless, peripatetic career. When World War I broke out, he moved to Fort Slocum, New York, to direct its hospital's psychiatric ward, then transferred to Advance General Headquarters in Trier, Germany, to study the effect of malnutrition on the mental development of German schoolchildren. From there it was on to London, to complete a diploma in neurology and psychological medicine, before returning to the United States for brief teaching stints at the University of Minnesota and Vassar—where with his wife, Margaret, he wrote dozens of articles on stammering and mental hygiene. In 1929 he left for Vienna to study with Freud and, during the summers of 1935–37, while the National Socialists took over the city, began a truncated psychoanalysis with him.

Drawing on Freud's argument that religion was a force and power, as well as a set of beliefs, the clinic and associated foundation that Blanton and Peale set up successfully addressed not just the anxiety of the times but also the widespread yen for self-improvement and the broad, unstinting faith in scientific progress. Peale's books were marketed to assure Americans "How Faith and Science Working Together Offer More Satisfying Answers to Everyday Situations."[53] His best-seller spawned a host of copies, such as Oral Roberts's *God's Formula for Success and Prosperity* (1955), and the creation, by the pastor of Manhattan's Fifth Avenue Presbyterian Church, of *Dial-A-Prayer:* "For a spiritual lift in a busy day."[54]

Under Peale's leadership, with encouragement from allies in Washington (including Eisenhower and Hoover) and across the business world, the American Foundation of Religion and Psychiatry helped to make psychiatry—and, briefly, the country as a whole—more religious. It did so, documents show, by asserting that religious belief was so integral to mental health that total psychiatric recovery was unlikely in a person who had not undergone full religious conversion. To concerned observers, this amounted to more than "tying psychiatric problems in with religious ones"; it wrongly led patients—and, by implication, the nation at large—to make religious faith essential medically.[55] To Peale and Blanton, by contrast, the foundation was helping the United States "combine the discipline of psychiatry with the profound influence of God."[56]

Perhaps unsurprisingly, given the interconnections, the meteoric rise of the foundation as a national organization influenced and in turn mirrored the spectacular rise of public religiosity across midcentury America. After eight years, the religious boom of the 1950s flagged, with plummeting trends in church attendance and other variables closely reflecting trends in religiosity.[57] Losing direction and funding shortly thereafter, the foundation eventually merged with the Academy of Religion and Mental Health, an ecumenical organization that had firmly rejected evangelicalism and religious conservatism since its creation in 1954. The academy also encouraged different ties between science and religion—ties based on limited but significant areas of overlap between the two areas, such as pastoral care.[58] Among other claims, it argued that religiosity was itself a reason for the continued general antagonism toward science and that religious moderation held the key to their reconciliation.

In reaction to the evangelicalism of ministers such as Peale and his foundation, the Academy of Religion and Mental Health departed from what it called "the rigidities of organized religion," warned of major differences between "mature" and "immature" religiosity, and tackled the risks and consequences of religious fanaticism. It studied the psychological advantages and drawbacks of religious faith and held symposia on how science and religion in the United States could be less adversarial. In the aftermath of the explicitly political religiosity of the 1950s, itself an outgrowth of the Christian nationalism of the 1930s and 1940s that Peale and his allies had done so much to foster, the academy integrated with Peale's foundation in 1972 to form the Institutes of Religion and Health. Thereafter a sponsor of interfaith research, it helped to redraw religious life in America by encouraging frank debate, embracing inquiry and ecumenical approaches, and stressing the need to end religious fanaticism.

The organizations at the center of this book are no longer household names (although Norman Vincent Peale may be). Yet the issues they raised and discussed are still making news. Some of the lines between science and religion have again become fraught, with hostilities on either side. Many among the country's leading evangelicals continue to insist that we live on a planet scarcely ten thousand years old, that climate science is hokum, and that dinosaurs and *Homo sapiens* once coexisted, more or less happily.[59]

Influential scientists such as the biologist Richard Dawkins, the neuroscientist Sam Harris, and the cognitive scientist Daniel C. Dennett have encouraged their own form of polarization. Dawkins has characterized religious people as "faithheads" and tried to argue away all distinction between faith and delusion, concluding that "faith is an evil."[60] In *The End of Faith*, though his position has since softened, Harris explicitly calls religious sentiment a form of mental illness, accuses moderates of complicity with fanaticism, and labels Christians "God's Dupes."[61] Meanwhile, in *Breaking the Spell*, Dennett lauds secularists as "brights" while casting religion as a parasitic "virus" and "toxic" spell.[62] In seeking to unwind decades of religiosity, these writers revert to early notions of religious belief as itself a form of illness.

Surge of Piety brings a fresh perspective to these conflicts. In it I trace some of these writers' animus against Peale's brand of Christian positive psychology and religious nationalism, his writing, and his evangelistic foundation, detailing how all of these elements incited a national religious revival.

Christian positive psychology transformed the nation's

religious landscape. Today's anxiety about secularism often returns evangelical Americans to the same concerns that roiled
the 1950s: the status of science, the power of religious faith,
the force of politics, and the combined effect of each on the
nation's most cherished notions and beliefs. Still, as we shall
see, the contemporary conflict between religion and science
could be lessened so that the extremes charted here might be
less of a presence in twenty-first-century America.

I

Religio-Psychiatry Arrives in New York

In 1937, near the depths of the Great Depression, when Peale and Blanton pooled their resources and opened a small clinic for the troubled and the needy, work was scarce and anxiety was widespread. Across the nation, wages and prices had slumped, and banks were failing with alarming frequency—an estimated four thousand of them in one year alone. Soup kitchens crowded New York City in response to the sharp rise in poverty and homelessness, and clusters of hastily assembled shacks—"Hoovervilles," named after the former president and his disastrous economic policy—dotted Central Park. Housed off one side of the Marble Collegiate Church, near a then-struggling midtown New York, the clinic sprang from an urgent need to help a city in crisis and a nation on its knees.

Daily confronting the suffering of his congregation and that of the city, Peale looked to psychiatry for help, only to face

a serious conundrum: religion and psychiatry had little in common. They approached and treated distress and mental illness
in quite different ways. A split in American culture had put
religion and the behavioral science in camps so far apart that
they could barely communicate. While psychiatry tended to be
broadly hostile to religion, dismissing it as retrograde and irrational, the kind of religion that Peale preached was less about
doctrine than about personal faith and conviction.

"In quiet rooms in the Marble Collegiate Church, shut
off from the brawling traffic of New York's Fifth Avenue," he
later announced from the more-prosperous 1950s, there stands
"a clinic where religion and psychiatry have, we believe, been
welded into a powerful therapy for the ills that wrack the
human spirit. Here, under the joint direction of a clergyman
and a psychiatrist, many harrowed men and women are learning to break down the barriers that keep them from living
successfully."[1]

To lessen anxiety and restore lost confidence, the Religio-
Psychiatric Clinic treated the distressed, whatever their financial resources; it grew into a national foundation—the American Foundation of Religion and Psychiatry—that distributed
brochures asking, "Why am I unhappy about myself?" As the
same literature made explicit, the foundation (with the clinic
proper as an integral but distinct part) also aimed "to encourage [patients] to accept religiously motivated ideas and ideals
as a means of solving personal problems."[2]

Funded initially by royalties from Peale's enormously
successful Christian self-help guides, the Religio-Psychiatric
Clinic was rapidly accredited, with research at the foundation
targeting larger, more-political matters of belief in self and
country. Both the clinic and the foundation aimed to discover
the "science of a satisfying life" and how Americans might be

EVERYONE HAS PROBLEMS—
What are you going to do about yours?

"Everyone Has Problems." Brochure for the American Foundation of Religion and Psychiatry, May 1960. Institutes of Religion and Health Records, Special Collections Research Center, Syracuse University Libraries.

encouraged to view religion as both a sign and a condition of mental health.[3] Affiliates of the foundation soon dotted the nation, with well-laid plans for comparable ones around the world. Arrangements were drawn up for meetings with the Archbishop of Canterbury and members of Westminster Abbey in London, officials of the American Cathedral in Paris, and prominent Lutherans in Berlin.[4] With characteristic enthusiasm and clear-eyed ambition, Peale's board took to calling the foundation "without a doubt the leading institution of its kind in this country—and probably [with] no equal anywhere in the world."[5]

Internationally known by the late 1950s as an advocate of positive thinking, Peale reached millions of Americans in promoting and celebrating the era's well-documented "surge in piety."[6] He called it a "great spiritual awakening" and claimed there was "a lot of religion involved in successful science."[7] His reach included national radio and television; his magazine,

Guideposts, also had millions of subscribers, including senators and a string of U.S. presidents.

Back in 1937, however, as the "fog of the Great Depression began to lift" (even as national unemployment climbed to
19 percent and beyond), the opening of the Religio-Psychiatric
Clinic was obviously a well-timed act of mercy.[8] "Everyone was
emotionally affected," noted one contributor to an oral history
of the period. "We developed a fear of the future [that] was very
difficult to overcome. . . . There was . . . this constant dread."[9]
Operated at the outset by a small, mostly unpaid staff, the
clinic was soon overwhelmed by large numbers of New Yorkers
in despair over lost work, lost savings, and the consequences
of both for their families and relationships.

That Blanton and Peale mentioned the clinic often in
their books—as a basis for anecdotes meant to inspire and
renew religious faith—helped to rapidly expand their client
lists.[10] *The Art of Real Happiness* (1950), their first co-written
book, opens with what amounts to an extended ad for the clinic
and its "faith-restoring process."[11] Peale also gave the clinic a
couple of prominent mentions in *The Power of Positive Thinking* for its enormous readership to see.

The American Foundation of Religion and Psychiatry
would document its aims, like its meetings, with scrupulous
care; its archive offers an intimate glimpse of its inner workings.
Yet there is little on the early years of the Religio-Psychiatric
Clinic, from which it sprang. What survives gives the impression of a small basement refuge—a warren of pint-sized rooms
off one side of the Collegiate Church, bordering West 29th
Street and Fifth Avenue. "People standing in knots on the cor-
ner spoke Yiddish and Italian as well as English," one observer
recalled. The church once towered over nearby buildings but

had become "boxed in among New York's garment lofts."[12] From the outset, the foundation (though not the church itself) was interracial in emphasis, which marked it as a brave outlier. The South was still formally segregated, not least in religious worship; the Supreme Court's ruling against segregated schooling, in *Brown v. Board of Education* (1954), was still two decades off.

Despite finding the science of psychiatry "religiously-antagonistic," Peale soon realized that his congregation's desperate plight raised issues far beyond his expertise. He contacted the secretary of the New York County Medical Association and asked him to "look for a psychiatrist to meet my specifications, a caring, well-prepared doctor, a Christian, one who could help a Christian minister." "He had to be a believer," Peale insisted, "and be of the highest professionalism."[13]

The recollection is Peale's, and the account almost apocryphal in his writing. Its frequent recounting helped to create a consensus that the two men, Peale and Blanton, were "true pioneers in the wilderness of mental illness."[14] They were quick to eulogize themselves, with Blanton calling their first lunch "the beginning of a turnaround ... [marking] the greatest advance in pastoral treatment in centuries."[15] Their thinking, however, was evangelical and thoroughly at variance with American psychiatry and general medicine. "There are both spiritual and pathological aspects to mental illness," according to one of their documents. "Thus treatment must be religious as well as psychological." Blanton was more colloquial but no less emphatic: "God heals the patient. I'm only His agent."[16]

The American Foundation of Religion and Psychiatry soon became the model, its executive director claimed, for initiatives under way in England, Germany, Sweden, and Finland. Its alumni were busy setting up additional chapters in India,

Japan, Australia, and New Zealand. For religio-psychiatry to prevail in "every . . . religious community in the nation," the same director urged, its advocates should "relate the work of the Foundation to the needs of" both corporate executives and religious leaders.[17] With his colleagues in full accord, that is what they set about doing.

The notion that Peale and Blanton were fearless pioneers doubtless inspired their staff. It also promoted an internal impression that the foundation was embattled—as if in need of protection from quizzical, semihostile scientists, including psychiatrists in thrall to the concept that mental sickness could be treated with almost forensic precision.

Contemporary reports from the influential Group for the Advancement of Psychiatry (GAP) lent some support to both points of view. An "objective critical attitude" should orient the field, the GAP asserted, but hostility toward religion was far from universal among psychiatrists.[18] Having contributed to a distinguished collection of essays assessing the status of "civilization in the United States" in 1938, the prolific psychiatrist-author Karl Menninger concluded a foreword to the book *Psychiatry and Religious Faith*, as if from a pulpit, by writing, "The basis of all religion is the duty to love God and offer our help to His children."[19] In the early 1950s another voice was added to the religious side of the discussion, that of an émigré Australian psychiatrist, who became an unlikely but enormously popular celebrity in the United States. "Dr. Fred C. Schwarz, noted surgeon, psychiatrist, and authority on the Communistic philosophy of Dialectical Materialism," as he described himself, formed the Christian Anti-Communism Crusade, a Los Angeles–based organization that "stressed the role that atheism played in the formation of Communist doctrines" and tried to convince Americans that Christians could not be communists.[20]

By midcentury, religious sentiment was on the upswing in the United States, its revival gathering remarkable energy and momentum in ways that pressed for both support and explanation from the scientific and psychiatric communities. Other charismatic evangelizers in the "peace-of-mind" movement—Rabbi Joshua Liebman, Bishop Fulton Sheen, and Billy Graham among them—joined Peale in championing religious faith as a precondition for health and well-being, making the appeal more generic and widespread.[21] Each could call on vast audiences, with millions tuning in weekly to hear their broadcasts, including forthright messages on piety and politics.[22] The intensity of Americans' religious enthusiasm may have startled psychiatrists and psychologists, but the cultural force it generated could not be disputed.

All the same, the notion that Peale and Blanton were embattled pathbreakers clashes with a number of biographical factors, not the least of them Peale's well-burnished connections to business leaders, senators, and the White House, plus a significant portion of the American public. With 4.5 million paid subscriptions by 1985, *Guideposts* had twice the readership of *U.S. News and World Report* and a million more than either *Newsweek* or *People* magazine.[23] Peale, as president of the American Foundation of Religion and Psychiatry, was positioned to promote a massive, if short-lived, religious revival in the wealthiest, most powerful country on earth.

Fresh from psychoanalysis with Freud, and armed thereby with insights, Blanton cheered the joint focus on religion and psychiatry as a way to find clinical solutions to Americans' widespread suffering. With an eye to promoting both the clinic and the foundation, he seems to have embraced Peale's self-appointed role as "God's salesman" and even accepted his upbeat "Thought Conditioners," a series of pamphlets encouraging spiritual uplift, even though many psychological and psychiatric experts claimed they were closer to self-hypnosis and autosuggestion.[24]

Blanton seems to have had no public or professional qualms about Peale's connections to political groups leaning far to the right. Among them were the Christian Freedom Foundation and the Committee for Constitutional Government, which Peale chaired for several years (1942–45). Such groups sparred with the federal government, which they thought both too secular and overly friendly to unions—or, in Peale's phrase, "indifferent to religion."[25] Viewing Christianity as an archenemy of communism as well as its best cultural defense, they promoted a staunchly conservative Christian vision of the country. Their aims were to end the New Deal, turn religion into a sturdy path to nationalism and personal fulfillment, and, above all, get Americans back into church.

Politically liberal, Blanton was viewed by at least some of Peale's supporters as "running around the country defending Communists," as one indignant woman complained in 1950.[26] After "soothingly talking about brotherly love and kindred themes," another audience member warned, he "suddenly lashed out a vituperative attack on the new law against communists," implying that opponents of the law were "martyrs to a national wave of witch-hunting!"[27]

The second complainant turned out to be legislative chair of Fort Worth Pro-America, whose members in the early 1950s were "pledged to fight against communism and socialism" in any and all forms—doubtless a factor in her reaction.

But Blanton was also criticized for trading on Peale's name. Conservative groups were puzzled by their close association. "Now, dear Dr. Peale, you are above reproach," wrote one. "We all revere you and are grateful for your teachings, which makes this subtle propaganda [from Blanton] all the more sinister."[28]

Peale was mortified by the complaints and apparently surprised by the described content of Blanton's ad-libs. He wrote a vigorous defense of his colleague, calling him "without any question one of, if not the best [gentleman] in the United States. . . . On the matter of politics, [however,] there could not be a wider difference."[29]

Blanton was not in the least bit secular. Nor was he an unbeliever, as the complainants and he himself sometimes implied. Although he was almost sixty before he became connected with a church (Episcopalian), he had been devout since childhood—a "hillbilly Methodist from Tennessee" was his joking self-description to Peale.[30] The man who would later tell Freud, "You must not think I am becoming 'religious,'" is also quoted in Peale's autobiography as having declared, "We must always work under the eaves of God's house, for He is the great Healer of His children."[31]

Naturally, the religiosity of the two leaders influenced the clinic and the foundation in many ways. When consensus on core goals and principles became necessary, a staff credo circulated. Its third entry read: "God, in His infinite wisdom, love and mercy, has the power, by His grace, to make man whole." Its first entry: "Dr. Norman Vincent Peale, Co-founder of the Foundation, has made a unique and permanent contribution to religion and mental health in our time."[32]

The clinic's Program of Dedication took place at the Collegiate Church. A further declaration of religious allegiance, it opened with a hymn ("Faith of Our Fathers"), followed by a "Service of Dedication" led by Peale. A second hymn concluded the event:

> May we ever, may we ever
> Reign with Christ in endless day![33]

"A religious approach is involved in all of our treatment," affirmed the director of clinical services in 1957.[34] Seven years later, that enthusiasm was undimmed, as the executive director reported: "The entire staff is deeply committed to its task of serving God through the ministry of counseling."[35]

In the same set of founding documents, Stephen Prichard, director of development, evoked an era before Galileo and the Italian Renaissance as a time when "the high priest and physician were once fused." The foundation, he explained, sought to reintegrate the two roles. "When psychiatric techniques are used by men of faith," he continued, speaking now of 1950s America, "it is possible to once again integrate the healing of the mind to the life of faith."[36]

That treatment increases health and, in so doing, raises faithfulness was one of the foundation's core beliefs. "To the lost sheep of the mentally ill," Prichard added, in a metaphor combining compassion for the sufferer with a hint of blame for their predicament, "love and understanding are the prerequisites to faith and reconciliation with God and fellow man."[37]

There are immediate, far-reaching consequences to making "reconciliation with God" a "prerequisite" to successful treatment and health—not just for individual patients but for the culture and the population at large, given the foundation's growing interest and influence in national debates. From the start, a patient's suffering and symptoms were put in religious

"Mental and Emotional Health." Poster for lectures sponsored by the American Foundation of Religion and Psychiatry Women's National Council, January–March 1959. Institutes of Religion and Health Records, Special Collections Research Center, Syracuse University Libraries.

terms, which makes the illness broadly inseparable from spiritual failing. The approach also ties recovery to religious atonement—rather than, say, to whatever strictly medical treatment is offered for tumors, flu, or failing organs. As Roland Reed, assistant director of training, explained when advocating a biblical understanding of health as spiritual soundness, "health" at the foundation was "used synonymously with salvation."[38]

Fred Tate, director of clinical services, spelled out how this "biblical understanding" was meant to work with patients: "Through 'transference' as we of psychiatry call it, our clients give up their bad images of a punishing and vengeful parent and God, and come to regard both parents and God as loving, accepting, and forgiving. The client is led, rather than directed, to this peace of soul. It is a conversion phenomenon, accomplished through transference, one of the most powerful instruments for healing."[39]

And if a patient was not devout? The doors of the Religio-Psychiatric Clinic were open to all, its literature stressed, and no one in need was turned away. Fees were set low and religious differences set aside in an atmosphere presented as warmly nonsectarian. Yet evangelism fills the clinic's pamphlets, not least in the idea that health springs from "reconciliation with God."[40] A foundation brochure advises patients both actual and prospective to have a religious outlook on life: "It is the broadly held belief among professionals in the field of mental health that the lack of a religious outlook on life is at the heart of many emotional problems." Though far from being a "broadly held" belief at the time, this was nonetheless an assertion that Peale and his colleagues worked hard to establish as consensus. An unnamed psychologist is quoted as reporting that "of his adult patients over 35 . . . 'none of

Most mental illness can be cured.

Serious mental illness can often be prevented by prompt treatment in their early stages.

The American Foundation of Religion and Psychiatry attempts to discover and treat emotional disorders not only at an early stage, but it has found that *more* effective relief results when these two disciplines of religion and psychiatry join forces. From the beginning the basic philosophy of the Foundation's work has been that *mental illness must be considered as reflecting a spiritual disturbance as well as a psychological or an organic pathology.*

Thus, treatment must be religious as well as psychological. By working together the clergyman and the psychiatrist can accomplish far more than either one can achieve alone.

"Most mental illness can be cured." Promotional brochure for the American Foundation of Religion and Psychiatry, late 1950s. Institutes of Religion and Health Records, Special Collections Research Center, Syracuse University Libraries.

them has really been healed who did not regain his religious outlook.'"[41]

That connection between religions and mental health becomes a bedrock theme in the case literature. When Peale and Blanton describe their patients at the beginning of *The Art of Real Happiness,* they call them "intelligent, well-disposed persons who had tried earnestly to follow their best ideals ... [b]ut somehow their religion had failed them; it had ceased to be for them a dynamic way of life." The aim of treatment, the minister and the psychiatrist write, is to restore in such patients "a vibrant faith" that will "give them confidence in themselves and trust in their Creator."[42]

There is no record of Peale's replying to a woman who

(his secretary advised) sent him "a bitter denunciation of God as a 'repeating hit and run driver.'" The woman had endured several eye operations over a short span, then lost her husband. "For myself my faith is blocked shut," she lamented. ("Shall I just file this, or do you want to answer it?" his secretary asks. "File.")[43]

Instead, the book's opening vignette is of a patient whose religious doubts Peale and Blanton seem rapidly to dispel. The young man, an architect, is said to "suffer . . . from a profound sense of impending disaster" and to live "in the shadow of an unrelenting anxiety." Although the brief portrait mentions a domineering and unpredictable father, its focus turns to the young man's religious skepticism. "By the time he came to the clinic," Peale and Blanton write, "he believed that he had even lost faith in God. 'God is a delusion,' he said during the first interview." But, they continue,

> as he gained insight into the true nature of his problem, a burning but hitherto completely repressed and hidden anger toward his father, a powerful mental catharsis [began to take] place. The rage that had been poisoning his mind was dissipated. And, after some religious guidance which revitalized his atrophied capacities for love, he not only shook off the painful anxiety which had tormented him since childhood, but he was also enabled to regain his lost faith in God and in mankind.[44]

Whether this patient actually existed, however—whether this and other published "cases" are factual reports or were adjusted or even greatly embellished—is in doubt. One of Peale's letters to Blanton suggests a degree of invention: "Enclosed are two or three case studies which I have roughly dashed off. Will you kindly read them over and if you think they have any possibilities, put the old master psychiatric touch on them."[45]

Whatever the "old master psychiatric touch" amounted to editorially, it is strange to think about "dashing off" an actual case history, given the need to present details accurately. Peale clearly felt no such constraint. The "cases" that he detailed share traits that are given to all such anecdotes in his books, including the patients' turn to piety following "religious guidance." They seem purpose-fit rather than genuine, with the first beginning characteristically: "A businessman who had not been in the habit of attending church came to our services . . ."[46]

At the Religio-Psychiatric Clinic, release from anxiety was not said to come—much less to last—without full faith in God. "Once the psychiatrist with his specialized skills begins the task of removing these neurotic barriers built of hate, resentment, fear, and anxiety," Peale and Blanton explain, "religious guidance then stimulates an influx of healing faith in the ultimate power and rightness of God."[47]

But if psychiatry could, on its own, remove "neurotic barriers," in what sense could "religious guidance" be thought necessary? For what was it here being used? Were Peale and his foundation merely helping their patients back on their feet, including through pastoral care, or were they misleading and potentially manipulating them, as some later charged, by insisting that religion was a precondition for their full recovery?[48]

On visiting the clinic in the late 1950s, Samuel Klausner, a researcher at Columbia University, described "chairs upholstered in orange plastic blend[ing] with pale blue walls and deep green carpeting. A secretary was scheduling appointments while a girl sobbed answers—name, place of birth. . . . An office suite adjoining . . . bore the sign 'Religio-Psychiatric Clinic.'"[49] Patients were routinely asked their "religious affiliation at present," with space for noting "changes made in past"—presumably, in denomination, baptismal status, and so on.[50]

Although the scene seems unexceptionable, the administrators worried: for the clinic to advance professionally it was "imperative" that it "have a clinic image."[51] Yet in terms of the sheer number of people passing through, the endeavor was inarguably a success: 7,100 patients were counseled between 1951 and 1956, a remarkable feat for such a small staff. During that time, the clinic also more than doubled the number of sessions it gave, from 2,400 hours to 5,600.[52]

Records show that depression and anxiety led among patient concerns, at respectively 60 and 50 percent of all described problems. The category "inferiority" trumped marital concerns (at 36 percent to 31), and "suspiciousness" as a behavior was somehow determined to be more prevalent a complaint than were sexual problems (respectively, 23.5 and 22 percent).[53]

Reports convey that the staff were kind and concerned. "Mrs. Elizabeth Ehling," wrote Klausner, "stood at the reception room door, smiled, and gently motioned woman and child down the corridor." The scene shifts to a snapshot of another staff member:

> Elizabeth Lyons was trying to boil water for instant
> coffee and gulp it down in the ten minutes between
> patients. Miss Lyons, a tall carrot-topped psychiatric
> social worker, complained about the mistreatment

CLIENT PROBLEMS

Presented to Clinic

of

AMERICAN FOUNDATION OF RELIGION AND PSYCHIATRY, INC.

PROBLEM	PERCENT OF ALL CLIENTS COMPLAINTS
1. Depression	60%
2. Anxiety	50%
3. Anger	38%
4. Inferiority	36%
5. Marital	31%
6. Work-Underproduction	30.5%
7. Withdrawn	24%
8. Suspicious	23.5%
9. Dependent	22.5%
10. Sexual	22%

"Client Problems Presented to Clinic of American Foundation of Religion and Psychiatry, Inc.," 1955. Institutes of Religion and Health Records, Special Collections Research Center, Syracuse University Libraries.

of patients in other clinics. Schizoid performing art-
ists were her specialty. One cried on the other end
of her telephone and she replied like a stern parent
to an unruly child. Her patients were encouraged to
organize a self-employment agency and to come to
an evening reading circle and Saturday teas.[54]

The emphasis on religion—muted in some staff; full-
throated in others—underlay all that the clinic strove to accomplish. "Hardly a day passes," Blanton noted in minutes,
"when [I do] not at some time ask God's guidance to help [me]
to help His clients."[55] His published writing was even more
emphatic: "Successful living hinges on the capacity to believe.
The unconquered and unconquerable of this world are those
who have mastered the art of faith." His private correspondence with Peale was candid in its assurances that training
classes taught at the foundation were strongly religious: "Everything is kept within the Christian tradition . . . there is no
over-emphasis on psychiatry."[56]

Given the clinic's and foundation's joint emphasis on
evangelizing, the notion that religious faith was valuable and
beneficial to the devout morphed quickly into the assertion
that it was essential for the health and harmony of all, to "restore" Americans' "faith in themselves and in God."[57] Privately
to Peale, Blanton enthused that one of Peale's "Thought Conditioners" had "worked a strange change in . . . a complete
Atheist." After about a month of treatment, she allegedly told
Blanton: "You know, Doctor, I am talking to the Rabbi now . . .
and really believe that there is a loving God on whom we can
depend."[58]

In the first decades of the twentieth century, psychiatry
had posited that mental catharsis alone was necessary for relief

from neurosis.[59] The development of this behavioral science is often described as stemming from its ability to emancipate itself from theological reasoning.[60] The ensuing divide helps to explain the standoff between psychiatry and theology. For Peale and Blanton, however, establishing in a patient a feeling of the "ultimate power and rightness of God" was "the driving force that motivates our entire program."[61] In proselytizing patients and Christianizing psychiatry, and medicine more generally, they were tailoring a message to support the national resurgence of piety: that a normal, healthy American was also, necessarily, a deeply religious one.

II

On the Couch with Freud

"The first step . . . toward the restoration of faith is to exorcise the devils of submerged emotional conflict."[1] If this sentence from Peale and Blanton's first book sounds like a strange blend of Christianity and Freud, that should not be altogether surprising. Blanton himself underwent a series of brief psychoanalyses with Freud, one beginning in September 1929 and lasting for almost a year and others during the summers of 1935, 1937, and 1938, with sessions at roughly two-week intervals.

Most of this analytic work predated the opening of the Religio-Psychiatric Clinic, and the clinic's practice came to rely strongly on it. As Blanton explains in a published diary, he often quizzed Freud about religious belief in their sessions, including how to enhance its psychological effects and what ends belief could be put to. Such was the detail of those exchanges, and Blanton and Peale's clear use of them in the years that followed, that the question arises: Did Freud, outspoken in his criticism of religion, inadvertently influence some of the thinking behind the postwar U.S. religious revival, including the major psychological and political forces that gave it strength?

Even though Blanton records quite intimate details in *Diary of My Analysis with Sigmund Freud,* including his own dreams and fantasies, what he initially wanted from Freud is enigmatic. "Did you come for any special reason to see me?" Freud asked in August 1937, shortly before anti-Semitism forced him to flee Vienna, at age eighty-two, to seek asylum in London.[2]

Freud's flight—protracted, stressful, and dangerous—involved ransom money, foreign diplomats, a former U.S. president (Woodrow Wilson), and the confiscation of property. His books had already been publicly burned in 1933, when the Nazis took control of Germany. As Blanton's wife, Margaret, explains in a note to his entries from 1938: "Menacing visits from the Gestapo, detention of his daughter Anna for interrogation, and robbery of his household funds by gangs of Storm Troopers had transformed the Nazi threat into an ugly reality for [Freud's] family as well as himself."[3] His four sisters would be murdered in the camps.

Although Margaret includes her husband in expressing concern about Freud during this hazardous time, he comes across as strangely detached, almost blithe, in his reply to Freud's question about whether he had a reason for coming: "No, I replied, no special reason, except for the general help you can give and the joy that the hours bring to me."[4]

That particular meeting gave Blanton a chance to talk about the clinic and to quiz Freud on spiritual healing and religio-psychiatry in a manner influential to the religious and clinical movement he would develop with Peale: "This was my last session. . . . I began by expressing the sadness I felt at having to go. Then I asked a couple of technical questions."[5]

In a preface to the *Diary*, published five years after Blanton's death in 1966, Margaret explains that after studying psychiatry at Johns Hopkins, then neurology and psychological medicine at the Royal College of Physicians and Surgeons in London, Blanton had "hoped to obtain the necessary additional training [in psychological medicine] by going to Europe and studying with Freud, if this could be arranged."[6] Later, in a biographical note, she confides that each of them underwent analysis (only her husband with Freud); and Blanton himself reports apprehension at the undertaking, making it clear that he preferred the generic and the technical to the personal.

Rather than undergo deep analysis, Blanton preferred to discuss broader, metapsychological issues, including best practices and Freud's thoughts on faith healing. His parting words to the professor, as he called him, sound closer to a course evaluation: "I did not get what I expected, which was advice about analysis and patients. But I got something better—a better knowledge of myself and a help in analyzing dreams."[7]

Early in the sessions with Blanton, Freud advises him, "It is better not to prepare what you are to say," for Blanton had a tendency to stick to talking points worked up the night before.[8] By the third session, with Blanton speaking more spontaneously, Freud notes courteously (in English, the language of their analysis): "You must follow the rule of analysis and be free to let your mind go as it will. Do not feel that you must keep along some preconceived path. You will probably get where you are going just the same."[9]

At that point, roughly midway through the *Diary*, the tone changes abruptly from partial self-reflection to full-blown

Smiley Blanton near the time of his analysis with Freud, c. 1935. Institutes of Religion and Health Records, Special Collections Research Center, Syracuse University Libraries.

tutorial, with Blanton primarily interviewing Freud and gathering professional advice. A raft of questions follows for much of the second half of the book: "I asked Freud what he would do if . . .'"; "I asked Freud if he advocated . . ."; "I asked Freud about his new ideas on . . ." The answers are enlightening, especially as snapshots of Freud's late thinking, but the questions mask Blanton and his intentions while drawing ever more attention to his enduring focus: religious faith and transference.[10]

When Blanton mentions his intention to visit Lourdes, in southwest France, and is asked if he is a Catholic drawn to the religious cures said to take place there, he responds: "No, I am nothing. . . . My religion is about like yours, as expressed in *The Future of an Illusion*. But I feel that average people cannot have such a bleak religion. Their minds are not well enough furnished. They must have an idealized father to depend on." Freud is noted as replying, "You are probably right."[11]

In Blanton's case, saying that his religion was "about like" Freud's was far from accurate. The psychiatrist who just three years later would co-write *Faith Is the Answer* and help establish the American Foundation of Psychiatry and Religion "under the eaves of God's house" steers the conversation repeatedly to faith and religion and brings large measures of both to their final sessions.[12] "In a democracy the citizen has certain inalienable rights given him by God Almighty," he asserts in their second-to-last meeting, "so that the Bible, in one sense, is the source of our democracy."[13] The comment is jarring, inaccurate, and, in the diary, comes out of the blue.

Before visiting Lourdes, Blanton jokes with Freud. "You must not think I am becoming 'religious.' Margaret is even more coldly scientific."[14] Even so, Freud's candid reaction to being asked repeatedly about the possibility of "miracle cures" upsets Blanton, to the point of generating tension in the same session. Couching the personal as technical, he writes of telling Freud, "Perhaps I am resentful in the unconscious that you do not accept my case of the Irish boy who was healed." He adds, sounding annoyed, "Perhaps I did not make it clear that he had records from three hospitals and that the doctors who gave him copies of the examination of his physical state did not know what might happen to him when he got to Lourdes."[15]

"Well," Freud reportedly answers, "I did not deny . . . that the facts were as [you] presented them." Indeed, his earlier response as to whether miracles occur at Lourdes had been, "As the Italians say, 'Perhaps no; perhaps yes.'"[16]

Freud's diplomacy left room for Blanton's religious beliefs. His reply also conceded that a strong *expectation* of cure could aid a patient medically. The placebo effect—a point of shared interest—would help explain why. (Current research suggests that telling a patient, "This *will* relieve your pain," works better than saying, "This *might* help.")[17]

But Blanton was irked at Freud's doubts about religious healing. He raised the matter several times, including as the basis of a recurring argument between Margaret and himself. When told of her emphasis on reason and probability, Freud reportedly replied, "I must take Margaret's side. . . . You have no right to believe because of ignorance. Of course, if people believe this or that in their private lives, I would not fine or punish them. But scientifically they have no right."[18] The notes for the session end there.

Blanton could not let the matter drop. He returned to it in a discussion of religious faith and the work then under way at the clinic in New York. He spoke of how he saw "patients who were referred to me by the minister, and of my plan to write a book with Dr. Peale—to write the psychiatric aspect of each subject (anxiety, alcoholism, etc.) and the minister to present his side."[19]

Phlegmatic about the collaboration, Freud was none-theless pleased about Blanton's professional development: The partnership "'gives you reputation,' he said in a tone of appro-bation."[20] But things did not go as smoothly when Blanton re-turned to the goals of psychoanalysis and religion. "It seems to me," he offered a week later, "that psychoanalysis tries to mod-ify our hate and aggression, and religion tries to do the same thing." This would be a key claim and platform for the clinic and the American Foundation of Religion and Psychiatry—one to which Blanton would hold for the rest of his career. The exchange faltered and ended cryptically in silence. "I don't know what you think of the comparison," Blanton pressed. "The professor made no reply."[21]

Although Freud and Blanton disagreed about the origins and motivations of religious faith, they shared a lively interest in its effects, both social and psychological. Each attributed the strength—even the tenacity—of faith to something called "transference"; the term comes up several times in their ex-changes. It refers to the intensity of affect, or sentiment, a per-son or element can elicit from another, especially during psychoanalysis. It encompasses our most childish and most resilient forms of attachment, from parental idealization to belief in religious healing and everlasting happiness.[22]

Far more strongly than Freud, Blanton thought that transference (including in its religious form) could hasten the healing process medically. His fascination with the idea was a key reason the clinic and the foundation threw their weight behind "spiritual healing," as part of a wider effort to promote "Spiritual Mobilization" across America. The idea was that religion and psychiatry worked in concert, bolstering a faith-inspired transference with the power to restore belief in health and ability, even to transform the thinking and mindset of a nation. (Spiritual Mobilization even became the name of one of the organizations Peale helped to administer.) As Blanton noted privately of one study of health and recovery that his colleagues consulted in the 1950s, it was "really a study of transference. Everyone knows that patients very often are healed with more rapidity because of transference to a doctor. . . . There is also transference to the Creator."[23]

Blanton and Peale had clear scientific pretensions for their work. They described the Religio-Psychiatric Clinic as "a scientific laboratory dedicated to the reshaping of men's daily lives." (Peale would also call the Bible "a book which contains a system of techniques and formulas . . . so precise . . . that religion may be said to form an exact science.")[24] And they were quick to recognize that transference might also revive, or generate, a form of religious sentiment with the power to influence behaviors and beliefs of groups large and small. This influence, in turn, would have far-reaching effects, not least for a people who, composing a "covenant" nation, would probably fight to defend those behaviors and beliefs, seeing them as inextricably bound up with their nation's history.[25]

In an essay on Lourdes, which goes into detail about how this process can work, Blanton writes of changes in patients that seem to occur "on the margins of the laws of nature." After particularly devout individuals visit Lourdes, a small town in the French Pyrenées whose spring water is the source of legends, many of them, he claims, experience a "quickening of the healing process."[26]

There in Lourdes, Blanton pored over the town's records, including those of a medical board that determines whether the health of previously ill patients deteriorates or improves. He concluded that the recovery reported to occur in a sizable number of cases was enhanced by "the emotion aroused by the transference to an all-powerful, all-loving Virgin Mother." He asserts that "to an extent which has not yet been realized or accepted by the medical profession," what he calls "some law of function" seems to alleviate symptoms in deeply religious patients—seems even in some cases to accelerate their recovery from chronic illness. He is also emphatic about the place of faith, as if continuing the argument with Freud. "No, these cures cannot just be thrown aside as imaginary, and the records, although not as perfect as one might wish, must be examined."[27]

Blanton's eagerness to study the intensity of the will to believe took him to the restorative power attributed to religious symbols and the role that such symbols can have in hastening recovery. According to him, the history of the sick-yet-devout turning to the Virgin Mary's shrine at Lourdes was closely aligned with a long history of mother-worship—a history that far predates Christianity. Given belief in the expectation of cure, there are striking psychological reasons why such a symbol could magnify the effects in a person already primed for an intense transference or placebo effect. As he explains,

> It is difficult for one not a Roman Catholic to realize how actual and real is the feeling of the believer for the Blessed Virgin. . . . The value of [her] as a transference object is infinite. No cross currents of human authority can touch her. She does not threaten, as a human mother does, even those who love her. On the part of the sick person the guilt payment has already been made by the act of being

so seriously ill. There is nothing in her love that can rearouse the sense of guilt.[28]

The case on which Blanton's article rests for evidence concerns a young man from Dublin, born in 1905, who in his twentieth year exhibited unmistakable signs of tuberculosis. In that the case gets to the heart of the debate between Blanton and Freud over religious transference and recovery, itself of broad significance to American revivalists and to Peale's American Foundation of Religion and Psychiatry, it is worth following closely.

The son of a carpenter, the young man, Charles McDonald, is treated for five weeks in an Irish sanatorium. His symptoms—night sweats, acute fatigue, and tuberculosis bacilli—abate, and he returns home to rest with his wife and children. Over the course of his six-month illness, his weight has dropped more than thirty pounds.

Feeling stronger and in need of work, he leaves for South Africa—first to recuperate, then to build frames for the mines outside Johannesburg. His health is stable for six years. But in January 1931, as a series of tests and X-rays confirms beyond doubt, his symptoms return.

Within a year, McDonald's health has deteriorated. His lungs too weak to tolerate an operation, he is put in an orthopedic brace and develops an abscess in the right lumbar region. By June 1935, two years before Blanton reads his case history in France, McDonald is back in Dublin with acute inflammation of the kidneys. He is admitted to a hospital after collapsing in "a violent fit of vomiting."[29]

During a two-month hospital stay aimed at stabilizing his health, "albumin, blood cells and granular and hyaline casts" routinely appear in his urine. The physician treating him quietly advises that he can do no more and recommends that McDonald "be transferred to the Hospital for the Dying." He returns home instead, where his wife dresses his wounds twice daily.[30] When not caring for him or their children, she tends a small fruit and tobacco store, their sole source of income, at the front of the house.

McDonald gives up hope that medical treatment can help him and instead comes to believe—Blanton claims to determine this from the papers—"that only by some divine intervention could he be helped." He arranges to travel to Lourdes, leaving Dublin on September 3, 1936. The nurse who dressed his wounds that night is on record as observing that there was "considerable pus draining from the sinuses in his back and shoulder."[31]

At Lourdes, on two consecutive days, McDonald is bathed in clean spring water that is locally considered holy. Blanton explains the town lore:

> On February 11, 1858, Bernadette Soubirous, a girl of fourteen who was being prepared for her first communion, saw in a niche above a grotto in the ancient rock, the Massabielle, an apparition of the Virgin Mother Mary. In all she saw this apparition nineteen times. During one of these visions she was directed to drink and to wash her face in a corner of the cave where she saw only mud. She dug with her hands and uncovered a spring at which shortly thereafter cures of a miraculous nature were reported.[32]

A half-century later, inspired by the legend of this impressionable girl, McDonald bathes in the spring but afterward is merely cold and numb. Several hours later, however, he is aglow and reports a rapid improvement, with pain diminishing in his back and movement returning to his arm. A day later, he is able to dress himself and walk to the end of his bed; this is the first time he has been on his feet in fifteen months. The day after that, he shaves himself, then leaves for Dublin. Without undergoing further bathing or treatment there, he returns to Lourdes shortly thereafter to report his changes. The town's independent board of physicians declares him completely free of tuberculosis bacilli. After McDonald returns once more to Dublin, one of the physicians who previously treated him also states, quite independently, "I have recently examined Mr. McDonald and found no active signs of his disease and as far as I can see he is completely cured."[33]

Blanton concedes that the water itself may yet be found to contain medicinal properties (none had been established at the time, he says, although a rumor to the contrary had circulated widely, doubtless influencing expectations). "But even if, for argument's sake, an unknown agency existed in these waters which acted as a specific, there is still the *rate* of cure and the comparative rapidity of convalescence to be explained."[34] Also notable, although Blanton quotes the patient without comment, is McDonald's striking reaction, after the second bath, to a slight freeing of movement in his arms and hips: "My expectations had become a certainty and the Blessed Virgin had healed me."[35]

"My expectations had become a certainty." Although Freud, accepting that transference could be elastic, could loosely agree with Blanton and Peale's "theory of the cure—that it was a transference to the ideal mother [via the Virgin Mary] which originated the impulse to live," he did not agree with Blanton's own suggestion that "psychoanalysis tries to modify our hate and aggression, and religion tries to do the same thing."[36]

While quick to concede that religion has a pastoral dimension, in caring for the sick and alleviating suffering, in such late works as *Civilization and Its Discontents* (1929) Freud viewed religion as a vehicle more for the expression of enmity and intergroup strife than for spirituality. As he noted of early Christian history and the beginnings of sectarian conflict, "When once the Apostle Paul had posited universal love between men as the foundation of his Christian community, extreme intolerance on the part of Christendom towards those who remained outside it became the inevitable consequence."[37]

Yet as Blanton himself noted in a later essay, "Freud and Theology," the American perception of Freud in the 1920s and 1930s as "an irreligious and even an anti-religious man" was not quite accurate.[38] Even though Freud in 1927 had explicitly called religion the "universal obsessional neurosis of mankind" and argued that it kept believers in a state of "infantilism," he also thought religion could serve as a "safeguard" against "certain neurotic illnesses."[39] In a cordial and lengthy exchange over religious faith with a Swiss pastor, whom at one point he called part of his family, he also identified himself as a "secular pastoral worker" offering an approach of enormous value to religious caregivers.

"In itself," Freud explained to the Reverend Oskar Pfister, "psycho-analysis is neither religious nor non-religious, but an impartial tool which both priest and layman can use in the service of the sufferer."[40] In *The Future of an Illusion* (1927), his critique of religious precepts, Freud outlined a point made in the correspondence: "If the application of the psycho-analytic method makes it possible to find a new argument against the truths of religion," that cannot be helped, "but defenders of religion will by the same right make use of psycho-analysis in order to give full value to the affective significance of religious doctrines."[41]

It is impossible to know whether Blanton had this passage in mind when asking Freud directly about the power of transference for therapeutic and religious ends, which he did before bringing out a book with Peale called *Faith Is the Answer*. Certainly Blanton had read *The Future of an Illusion* closely, as noted in his *Diary*. It is also obvious that he visited Freud convinced that the ardor of devout Catholics for the Virgin was a transference with life-altering, and possibly nation-altering, potential.

Blanton may have taken the argument further than Freud ever would have, but Freud had drawn attention repeatedly to the power of transference, calling it both "the condition of lasting success" in analysis and the mechanism serving "a profession of *lay* curers of souls who need not be doctors and should not be priests."[42] He warned of the risks of making excessive promises to patients (as he thought religion did), of telling them that they could look forward to complete freedom from suffering, immediately or eventually. He also noted the risks and temptations of playing God thereby. As he had put it wryly to Pfister, "Our patients have to find in humanity what we are unable to promise them from above and are unable to supply them with ourselves."[43]

"If I could, I should gladly do as others do and bestow upon mankind a rosy future," he had added, "and I should find it much more beautiful and consoling if we could count on such a thing. But this seems to me to be yet another instance of illusion . . . in conflict with truth. The question is not what belief is more pleasing or more comfortable or more advantageous to life, but of what may approximate more closely to the puzzling reality that lies outside us."[44]

The religiosity that Freud saw as resurgent in the United States, fueled in part by the efforts of Blanton's soon-to-be colleague, Norman Vincent Peale, suggested to the psychoanalyst that America was being "surfeit[ed] with piety" for social and political ends. He thought there were strong political incentives for "pious America" to again lay "claim to being 'God's own Country.'"[45] Of the temperance movement that Peale helped bring to power in Ohio, he wrote: "That the effect of religious consolations may be likened to that of a narcotic is well illustrated by what is happening in America. There they are now trying . . . to deprive people of all stimulants, intoxicants, and pleasure-inducing substances, and instead, by way of compensation, are surfeiting them with piety."[46]

Peale himself had been active in the National Prohibition Emergency Committee. As a minister in Syracuse, he had campaigned for years against newspapers, in particular, for undermining Prohibition. He was one of several rising religious stars who, in the words of one historian, viewed Prohibition as a "cultural struggle" for the nation—"as much a religious as a social-political crusade."[47]

Since Peale would later found with Blanton a Religio-Psychiatric Clinic and an organization aimed at fusing religious and psychiatric practice nationally, the fact that Blanton quizzed Freud about the potential religious direction of transference only adds to the irony of the situation, making us wonder whether Freud had been misled. Certainly, had he lived to see the way Blanton and Peale applied his counsel in the 1950s—by rendering faith a prerequisite for health, for example—the outcome would doubtless have appalled him.

Considering Blanton's and (to a lesser extent) Peale's debt

to Freud, we are nonetheless led to consider that psychoanalysis —and, to an extent not yet appreciated, Freud himself—played a larger role in America's postwar religious revival and its transformative religiosity than Freud could ever have wanted or imagined.

During one session with Freud, Blanton was encouraged to lessen his anxious concern about his patients' spiritual direction. "You must let them drift," Freud is reported to have advised him. "Let them work out their own salvation."[48] But Blanton was scarcely interested in taking religion out of clinical treatment, much less in loosening the ties between psychiatry and religion. On the contrary, he wanted more religiously inflected treatment to occur, and for religion and science to be fused and thought inseparable.

The twists and turns of the story continue. After an English rector and psychoanalyst brought out a book on Freud and Christianity in 1949, arguing that psychoanalysis showed "there is no special religious instinct," Blanton gave it a glowing review in the *New York Herald Tribune,* but he completely recast its thesis. There was now, as Blanton saw it, despite personal experience to the contrary, a "Dr. Freud for the Pulpit."[49]

Roy Stuart Lee, the author of *Freud and Christianity,* the book in question, wanted religion to be freed of unconscious fixations, and believers helped by psychoanalysis to demystify those fixations, but Blanton found the book better suited to showing how psychoanalytic techniques could strengthen religious faith. As Blanton reshaped the message, the Freud whom he knew personally to be sharply critical of religion is turned, incredibly, into a proselytizer for Christianity. "With this love of God in the heart," Blanton writes of eros, upending the term's Freudian meaning, "the aggressive, selfish impulses can be modified and sublimated to useful ends," including "in the 'Church Militant' to fight evil and cruelty."[50]

Similar observations on the power of religion influenced *Faith Is the Answer: A Pastor and a Psychiatrist Discuss Your Problems,* which Peale and Blanton published in 1940 and revised and expanded twice at the height of the religious revival. "It should no longer surprise anyone," they declare briskly in the opening to a later edition, "that a minister and a psychiatrist join forces in writing such a book as this, for in both spheres of activity the objective is essentially the same: the renewal of faith when faith has been lost—faith in oneself, faith in one's fellow man, and faith in God."[51]

That "faith in God" could end a sentence about, in part, the aims of psychiatry *as a science* helps convey both the religious confidence of the time and the fierce commitment of Blanton and Peale to making piety a precondition for mental health. "If there is a lack of faith in ourselves and in others and, ultimately, in God," Blanton preaches in his opening paragraph, "the time has come to take stock. For faith can mean fruition in the emotional as well as spiritual sense. Without it we are nothing."[52] Later in the book Peale insists that the ability to enjoy life is "a direct product of the Christian way of life." To cap the argument, he and Blanton even give the full address of the clinic where Americans could find their way to this panacea.[53]

How Christianity could orient psychiatry in treating mental suffering and illness, Peale and Blanton implied, was by turning faith into a medicine. To do that, however, was also to turn suffering into a disease that is religiously inflected. Peale writes of faith as if he were writing copy for Madison Avenue: "Its penetrating potency drives deep into those areas of the subconscious where lurk the sources of infection. It hunts down these mental disease germs and destroys them with the powerful heat of its clean life."[54]

From that supposedly scientific perspective, any element of illness, mental or otherwise, can be made into a symptom of sin or religious failing. Such an approach makes compassion for suffering inseparable from veiled or even explicit judgment about its apparent cause. During one prayer meeting that Peale and Blanton write about, a woman who has an epileptic fit is counseled that she has only "'pseudo' epilepsy." She routinely endures three seizures a day, the central cause of which, they claim, is that she is hostile to others. "She was made to realize that prayer would not help her until she could face this basic problem. When she achieved this, she was shown how to pray effectively."[55]

Techniques for effective prayer were addressed in a thoroughly scientific and highly directed way. "Set up for yourself your own laboratory for sustained research in prayer," Blanton and Peale exhort. "Pray at specific times. Be regular. Have a specific purpose for your prayer."[56]

To the author of a letter to his *Look* magazine column, asking for help for being "homosexually inclined," Peale offered hope. He wrote that the man was suffering from "an emotional sickness" and that "depth psychology has worked out effective methods of treatment for such trouble." "Consult a good psychiatrist," he advised. "If you prefer, the American Foundation of Religion and Psychiatry in New York, where psychiatrists and ministers work together, will be glad to help you, or any reader of *Look*, regarding any personal problems free of charge."[57] Waves of correspondence followed, leading to a sharp rise in the number of patient visits.

There could be no doubt about the type of advice they would receive. Given Peale and Blanton's joint emphasis on evangelical Christianity as psychiatric medicine and science, their book's carefully tailored anecdotes and "case studies" all point in the same direction: toward the need for religious faith. They quote one woman's letter to Peale:

> I am an average woman with the usual amount of ability and the usual amount of courage; but I am utterly discouraged now about myself. . . . My husband says I need a psychiatrist; my friends say I need a minister. But what in the world can religion do for a person who is just in a state of confusion and discouragement?[58]

Since the question invites the religio-psychiatric reply, the letter looks fabricated.[59] The woman, dubbed Mrs. A., is advised to attend the clinic, to consult both a minister and a psychiatrist. Yet she voices a high level of "discouragement" about herself, so it is striking that religion enters the advice picture at all.

By turning religious faith into a condition for belief in oneself and others, Blanton and Peale found a way to harness religion to psychiatry, to make piety and personal recovery inseparable. At the same time, they made the integration of religion and psychiatry seem natural and inevitable, on terms oriented to evangelical Christianity. The partners' Depression-era clinic quickly expanded, filling both a need and a niche among desperate, impoverished New Yorkers. It became the practical arm of an organization whose self-appointed mission was a renewed Christianizing of America, with links via Peale to corporations and conservative advisors across the nation. As its executive director would declare, its reach and influence extended to "religious leaders in every phase of the religious community of the nation."[60]

Eager for Americans to embrace Christian beliefs, Blanton—the psychiatrist who had once told Freud "You must not think I am becoming 'religious'"—joined an upbeat Norman Vincent Peale in calling for the "Church Militant" to have a greater cultural presence in the United States and the world.[61] With lack of "faith" designated one of the country's major ailments, religio-psychiatry would soon be branded the source of the cure.[62]

III

From Acute Shyness to "World Conquest"

While Blanton oversaw the day-to-day running of the clinic, Peale turned his attention outward, to mass counseling and to conservative groups aimed at Christianizing America. By 1940, he had speaking commitments stretching months, even years, ahead, and was throwing apparently limitless energy into pursuing his ministry, amplifying his public profile, and carrying out his work for the nation at large. He was rapidly making a name for himself in prominent circles, particularly among conservative Christians eager to make piety a sign of the country's long-awaited recovery from the Depression and religion a shield against its antidemocratic enemies.

A surge in public religiosity, it was claimed, would rejuvenate the nation and herald its full return to preeminence.[1] A mass "return to God" would also, Peale asserted, strengthen the population by "inoculating" it against communism—which, because of communism in the USSR (Stalinism in particular), had been cited since the mid-1930s as a threat to the nation's core beliefs.[2] For Peale, the question "Christ or Marx?" summed up a "perilous" dilemma. With "millions espousing [Marx's] ideals with fanatical zeal," he warned in October 1948, in a political sermon he titled "Democracy Is the Child of Religion," freedom itself was threatened. Religious belief was, by contrast, the "best way to preserve" freedom and was, accordingly, the very principle on which America needed to "crusade." The evangelical thrust was, for Peale, a consequence of standing united in steadfast opposition to forces such as collectivism. "Thus you have the issue," he summed up: "Christ or Communism, Christ or chaos, Christ or catastrophe, Christ or the police state."[3]

As minister of one of the oldest churches in New York City, Peale was exceptionally well placed to promote such assertions, to make being unreligious seem unbalanced, fanatical, and wholly "un-American."[4] He took on the task with relish, using his pulpit to lob almost weekly tirades at Washington.

With the national press riveted by Peale's every move, he became a lightning rod for national conservative concerns, from the sale of liquor to the perceived threat of labor unions, the godless, and the "alien, un-American ideologies" that, in his view, were behind the threat.[5] When he later took to radio and television and wrote a syndicated column, he reached even greater numbers with his message. Anticommunism was to Peale and his allies a pro-Christian stance, even if the religious component was not strictly necessary for the critique to hold. Aware of Freud's insights into the nature of religious enthusiasm, Peale knew that fervor could fire up Americans beyond the pulpit, especially when packaged as a promise of national renewal through personal and religious redemption.

"It is increasingly evident," he was quoted in the *Herald Tribune* as asserting, "that the only solution to the present [national and international] crisis is a deeper, more spiritual, more social Christianity." Even more, he urged—in the kind of accusatory turn that made him popular among hard-liners adopting the same refrain a decade later during the McCarthy hearings on un-American activities—"the man who shows no interest in Christianity and fails to support it is the real enemy of our social institutions."[6]

For those who know Peale from his most popular books it can be disconcerting to realize how thoroughly politics imbued his early sermons, talks, and religious activities. Especially in the late 1930s and early 1940s, when Peale was burnishing his reputation as a minister and speaker not just in New York but nationwide, his crammed press folders report the activities and accusations of a man with an extraordinary appetite for political conflict.

Peale's religious and psychological message blended affirmative prayer with practical self-help, in what has been called a "gospel of personal religion" and, more crudely, "God and gumption."[7] In combining these elements, he signaled with Blanton a strong desire to fuse theology with psychiatry and positive psychology, especially in connection with the power of belief ("faith in faith"). Yet he differed from Blanton in both the scale of his political vision and his willingness to inveigh at others who failed to share it. While many newspaper headlines hinted at an emphasis that he and Blanton shared—"Dr. Peale Sees Faith as Source of Power"—others skewed to a darker worldview: "Dr. Peale Sees Freedom and Faith Periled." The minister laced his message with drama to heighten a sense of urgency: "Christianity Seen in Race with Chaos," the *New York Times* reported of one such sermon, given long before America became embroiled in the Second World War, and continued with: "Final Destiny of Civilization in Our World Is the Prize, Dr. N. V. Peale Declares."[8]

When the country struggled to shake off the Great Depression, including through public works projects financed by the New Deal, Peale was especially active in hard-line lobbying groups whose self-appointed mission was to question the New Deal's very existence, to undermine it even by smearing its prime White House advocate, Franklin D. Roosevelt. The president was targeted despite his notable religious rhetoric. Roosevelt's first inaugural address was so "laden with references to Scripture" that it prompted the National Bible Press to release a chart highlighting the "Corresponding Biblical Quotations"; in his second inaugural address, in January 1937, he likened himself to "a modern-day Moses leading his people out of the wilderness."[9] Peale was unpersuaded. One newspaper article, after declaring, "New Deal Assailed as Curb on Reform: Dr. Peale Charges Hasty Moves for Selfish Ends Impede Real Social Progress," captures the flavor of Peale's blunt attack: "Ill-Conceived Experimentation Makes Public Wary of Progress, He Warns."[10]

In the *New York Sun*, Peale's target shifted once again: "Peale Assails Class Conflict: Criticizes Methods Used by Roosevelt." In this piece the New Deal was held virtually responsible for the mass inequality that Congress had hoped to reduce by passing a raft of crisis-stamped bills and reforms. The message was unmistakable, and the *New York American* spelled it out: "Dr. Peale Asks America to Put Roosevelt Out. Country Must Change Him or Change Constitution, He Declares in Sermon."[11]

It was in alluding repeatedly to the president's irregular

church attendance, however, that Peale found the political vul-
nerability that suited him as a minister. "Criticizes Roosevelt's
'Indifference to Religion,'" the *Herald Tribune* notes. "Dr. Peale
Calls It Cause of Vital New Deal Errors." Peale was particularly
aggrieved by the president's "Sabbath excursions and fishing
trips," although the relationship of these jaunts to seeming
mistakes in the New Deal remains far from clear. President
Roosevelt was, Peale said of a conflict over Supreme Court
appointees, "a presumptuous seeker after improper power." In
yet another political sermon, he warned ominously of the government's growing tendency toward "autocracy" and the president's tendency toward "dictatorship": "We can pull him down
when we wish."[12]

Peale's cheery autobiography and popular books on positive
thinking are carefully shorn of this amply documented history.
When it mentions Roosevelt, the autobiography admiringly
invokes the president's famous dictum, "The only thing we
have to fear is fear itself," and otherwise celebrates the America
of the time as "simple and homey, yet already bursting with the
excitement of an incredible future."[13]

Yet as Peale's clippings and correspondence reveal in impressive detail, his political activities dovetailed with his pitch
for a national religious revival, with Peale serving as both its
advocate and its partial figurehead. His repeated, enthusiastic
politicization of his ministry lent shape and force to the revival, given his outsize role as its popularizer.

Though far from original, and rapidly adopted by other
conservative revivalists, such as Billy Graham, Peale's claims
that faith in God, country, and self were broadly identical ac-
quired importance by dint of their enormous popularity in

postwar America. By 1955, *The Power of Positive Thinking* had sold almost a million copies and was outselling all other books except the Bible.[14] As his biographer Carol V. R. George concluded, "It was Peale's message that gave definition to the religious revival" of the early 1950s.[15]

Peale's conservative populism "surfaced in his partisan activities over the years," George continues, "and because the press gave generous coverage to his political views, he was constantly being sought out by individuals with political axes to grind." She claims that in his spirit of eager, voluntary participation, "he often jumped on bandwagons whose real destinations he did not know."[16]

Though much of that last claim remains doubtful, Peale's association with such far-right organizations as the Committee for Constitutional Government, Spiritual Mobilization, the Christian Freedom Foundation—and, briefly, H. L. Hunt's Facts Forum—sometimes generated enough controversy to be acutely embarrassing to him. When a book on hard-line conservatives appeared in 1943, noting accurately that Peale had shared a platform with Elizabeth Dilling and the Reverend Edward Lodge Curran, the damage to his reputation was considerable. Dilling, "a person the federal government ranked among the worst hate-mongers," was, notes George, "a 'patriot' who smeared liberals, Jews, African Americans, and other ethnic groups with the same broad brush."[17] Curran, founder of the National Committee for the Preservation of Americanism, was the author of such alarmist books as *Spain in Arms: With Notes on Communism* and *Facts about Communism*.[18]

Under Cover, which had been published by the Armenian American journalist Arthur Derounian under the pseudonym John Roy Carlson, was supposedly an exposé of "the

Nazi Underworld of America." In it Peale was cast as a patsy for the right—as a "docile Protestant clergyman" who chaired the rigid Committee for Constitutional Government while its executive secretary, Edward Rumely, was under Senate investigation for failing to disclose its murky sources of funding.[19]

With the *New York Times* and other prominent newspapers calling *Under Cover* "of sensational importance," Peale was quick to downplay broader involvement.[20] Privately he wrote to the author and his publisher, insisting that his reputation had been unfairly maligned.[21] Behind the scenes, however, he tended to respond with alacrity to such challenges, adjusting his emphasis to suit audience and occasion. A brief from Rumely for a 1943 meeting of the New York Economic Club explains, "Dr. Peale is supposed to touch upon the spiritual outlook ahead, which can mean the tracing of our institutions of freedom and free enterprise and constitutional government and their perpetuation in the post-war period." The memo continues: "Dr. Peale asks for suggestions of material and viewpoint that it would be desirable for him to bring out from this platform under this title."[22]

All told, the idea that America needed a pro-Christian nationalism to head off an attack of atheistic communism was central to Peale's message, and he stuck to it zealously. In 1947, four years after the *Under Cover* controversy flared, he could still enthuse to the conservative businessman Edward F. Hutton that "'Americanism or Communism' is one of the best you have done." He was referring to a half-page ad that Hutton had taken out in the *New York Times,* which among other things warned, "Communism will wipe out all we hold dear: God, family, country, liberty and possessions."[23] Related ads by Hutton for the Committee for Constitutional Government cried: "Help Rekindle Faith, Flaming Zeal In Our Constitution! Teach

"Help Rekindle Faith, Flaming Zeal In Our Constitution!" Advertisement by the Committee for Constitutional Government, Inc., c. 1947. Norman Vincent Peale Papers, Special Collections Research Center, Syracuse University Libraries.

Norman Vincent Peale in the 1940s.

the Value of Our Constitution and Its System of Free Enterprise to Youth Everywhere."

The Manichean thinking was clumsy but—for several years at least—highly effective, and Peale was candid in how it was meant to work, as he explained to Hutton.

> I believe that one of the best ways to undercut Communism is to reach the masses of the people with some simple religious principles. Not long ago I talked with a great Negro leader and asked him how we could stop Communism from making inroads among the colored people. He said that there is only one way to do that—keep the colored people strongly Christian. He said, "If a man has strong religious feelings he will repel such materialistic and godless philosophy." Communism can only take root in a soil from which the religious ingredient has been weakened or withdrawn. I think this also applies to the laboring people.[24]

The letter offers a clear, if hardly exceptional, summary of Peale's understanding of religion's political value. Elsewhere, in response to a correspondent's asking if President Eisenhower, later a friend and personal ally, might not be persuaded to ask the entire nation to engage in simultaneous prayer—Eisenhower had inaugurated a series of presidential prayer breakfasts, some on the theme of "Government Under God"—Peale wrote: "I am sure he would cooperate with the various denominations if they took the initiative. . . . Religious groups, however, have not fully realized the amazing power that is present in a group where all are thoroughly united in prayer."[25]

To Hutton in 1947, Peale added revealingly that with a
small group of like-minded Christians he had started

> a pamphlet service called GUIDEPOSTS in which we
> get outstanding businessmen, industrialists, sports
> figures, and others to write simple little articles
> about how religion has helped them. We . . . are
> sending out thousands of copies of these every
> month. At the present time many firms and in-
> dustries have their entire list of employees on our
> circulation list. 26,000 industrial foremen are re-
> ceiving it. Our purpose is to put it in the hands
> of everybody in the country who might possibly
> be receptive to Communism. We believe that in
> so doing, we are inoculating these people with a
> healthy mental spirit that will resist the disease
> germ of Communism.

The letter concludes with an appeal for "the very close tie-up
of freedom and religion." This, indeed, is the claim that Peale
credits to Rumely, still under Senate investigation: "Freedom
is the child of religion."[26]

Rather than limiting freedom through an array of commandments, laws, and injunctions, religion is here viewed as
giving birth to free thought, the Enlightenment movement
that historically fought to wrest sciences such as geology from
theology, to show, for example, that planetary history aligned
with the opening verses of Genesis, but only as poetry.[27] After
calling for "a resurgence of the spirit of religion" as "the best
way to preserve freedom," Peale asserted: "Every student of
history knows that Democracy is the child of religion."[28] Even
though the claim is far from accurate, whether in reference to

classical Athens or the age of Thomas Jefferson and Adam Smith, Peale's letter to Hutton ends by declaring that both democracy and religion are besieged and facing a "battle [that] cannot be fought alone with political mechanisms. We have to go deeper, so we must muster every force possible."[29]

Though privately expressed in this case, Peale's politics led him to take public stands and positions that made others, including clergy, leery of supporting him. One political action committee member warned that before he could endorse *Guideposts,* Peale would need to "free his ministry . . . from the compulsions of redbaiting."[30] A minister voiced concern about how far he was politicizing his ministry, despite Peale's assurance that "there is absolutely nothing political about *Guideposts.*"[31]

Certainly the pamphlets stuck mostly to religious and self-help themes, conveyed in a language of science and individualized fulfillment: "Down-to-Earth Gospel and Modern Science Clasp Hands and Change Lives on New York's Rich, Fashionable Mammonish Fifth Avenue," one brochure for Marble Collegiate Church put it, somewhat confusingly.[32] The emphasis on self-help was strikingly similar to that adopted months later by the Advertising Council for its highly successful and influential "Religion in American Life" campaign of 1949, during which Americans in large numbers were urged: "Find yourself through *faith.* Come to church this week."[33] Yet most reader requests for reprinted articles of *Guideposts,* George notes, were for "a 1948 piece by ardent Cold Warrior J. Edgar Hoover." And when a reader wrote canceling his subscription because he was "shocked at your Communist attacks," a forthright editorial offered the rejoinder: "We print and shall continue to print Communist exposures because Communists are Anti-God, Anti-Christ. . . . *Guideposts'* policy is in no way political."[34]

All the same, Peale privately conceded to Hutton that *Guideposts* had been designed all along to be "put . . . in the hands of everybody in the country who might possibly be receptive to Communism." The increase in mass subscriptions, including from allies in the business world agreeing to sign up their entire workforce, gave Peale an audience far beyond his church. "We hope to reach every teen-ager in the land," he noted elsewhere of another key demographic, in a similar revelation of his thinking and process. "We feel a deep sense of urgency and hope to plant in the minds of teen-agers the realization that the way to a happy, useful life is by sound, Christian morals."[35]

Peale's larger audience magnified the cultural and political sway he could count on newspapers to report, particularly if he found a way to needle someone prominent, such as the president. By serving at the same time as "God's salesman," he played a major role in promoting the nation's religious revival.[36] With other key figures, from Billy Sunday to Billy Graham, Peale encouraged Americans to view secularism as a scandalous "indifference to religion"—a form of godlessness that he denounced as un-American, antidemocratic, and deeply betraying the nation's history.[37]

America's postwar religious revival could profit handsomely from the country's deep-seated concerns about communism, Peale enthused. With *Guideposts* helping to "refertilize the soil of American life by widely spreading religious ideas [to] counteract the communistic virus," he was quick to criticize mainline clergy for appearing unduly hostile to private enterprise—and hence antidemocratic and pro-communist.[38] "Church Seen Confusing Its Creed with Socialism," the *Herald Tribune* dutifully reported. "Dr. Peale Says Christ Did Not Oppose Capitalism."[39]

In a controversial article Peale published in *Reader's Digest* in 1950, he addressed the problem directly, as the title makes clear: "Let the Church Speak Up for Capitalism."[40] He went on the CBS television program *Strike It Rich* on behalf of the American Foundation of Religion and Psychiatry. (The foundation minutes duly record that "a donation from the program of $500 is assured.")[41] He sprinkled his sermons and articles with advice from business-friendly research such as that collected in *Gaining the Clergyman's Understanding* (1951), on how to convert America's ministers from the so-called Social Gospel of the New Deal to the virtues of free enterprise.[42] He also cast aside any pretense at writing nonevangelical psychology, publishing books with titles like *The Coming of the King; The Positive Power of Jesus Christ; In God We Trust;* and *Sin, Sex and Self-Control.*[43]

What made the church attractive in its fight against communism, Peale reasoned, was that it gave individual Christians a major role in an increasingly impersonal, Manichean world. If the church could be presented as more affirmative than judgmental, he thought, it would share a message from religious conservatives that from other quarters would have seemed overtly political; it also would gain the trust of those already buffeted by fear and anxiety over world conflict and the measures (such as nuclear armament and the hydrogen bomb) then debated as necessary to address it.[44] Communism, forthright in its desire to eliminate both capitalism and the governments seen as supporting it, cast doubt on the ostensibly noble origins of the human race and dismissed religious faith as a mass distraction.[45] Both the Soviet Union and China (the latter by then in the early 1950s, under the control of communist leader Mao Zedong) had major weapons and armies of their own and were candid in their desire to attack and annihilate

American capitalists. Since millions of their own people had died (USSR), and would die (China), from harsh government measures, the danger to noncitizens had to be considered dire.[46] The world situation was even riskier because, as Ira Katznelson notes, the Soviet Union had felt threatened by the Truman Doctrine, opposed the Marshall Plan, and bristled at what would in fact be the creation of "a massive and permanent national security state" under Presidents Truman and Eisenhower.[47]

"When communism destroys the value of the individual and levels him down to a dull mass," Peale had averred in the late 1930s, "Christianity still sings of the nobility of every man."[48] To be an advocate for such nobility, even when history and science contradicted it, was to be energetically pro-Christian, pro-American, and pro–private enterprise ("I believe that Christianity has a considerable stake in the survival of capitalism").[49]

By 1950, after yet another conservative activist had written asking for Peale's support, he could candidly reply: "I've determined that for my part I'm going to vigorously fight Communism and all its works." The only surprise of such a statement, given the minister's activism over the previous two decades, is the impression he gives of a change in direction.

The man soliciting his support, Morton R. Cross, hoped that Peale would join him in arguing that in America "every strike is inspired by Communism." Although Peale wavered and finally demurred, thinking the claim overly broad, he assured Cross that he was "thoroughly in agreement with the idea that there is a strong Communistic impulse behind the labor union movement."[50]

That statement resulted in a follow-up the next day, with

Cross eager to give Peale "a few ideas" for future sermons and talks, should the need ever arise:

1. Is Truman supporting Communism?
2. Communism vs. Christianity.
3. Stalin controls his election by force.
4. Truman buys his votes through backing the Unions.

The Unions are controlled by a few leaders who:

a) Rule by intimidation;
b) By adopting unfair methods;
c) By disobeying laws;
d) Have the backing [of] and are defended by Truman;
e) There is no Christianity whatsoever in the methods they use.

In short, Cross hoped that Peale might be persuaded to imply that "Truman professes Christianity but defends Communistic principles."[51]

Although Peale stopped short of making personal attacks on Truman, perhaps remembering the consequences of his broadsides against Roosevelt, Peale had made quite similar claims about labor unions since the Depression, with newspapers reporting wild assertions, as here: "Dr. Peale Warns Labor to Be Wary of Betrayal. 'Sit Down' Strike a Communist Import." From Ireland to India, passive-resistance movements challenging British imperialism had been active since the eighteenth century. But Peale's point was to connect labor disputes with communism, to tar them with the same brush. As the *New York Times* put it, "Labor Is Warned of 'Foreign' Taint. Peale

Fears 'Red' Aspect of Agitation Is a Token of Un-American Trends. Deplores Bitter Spirit."[52]

Going to church, by contrast, implied a national pastime both "simple and homey"—and one uniting Americans in "spiritual renewal." Christianity, as Peale broadcast and published nationwide, tying religious belief to positive psychology, was "coming to be more widely recognized every day as possessing the surest techniques for helping people realize themselves."[53] Despite sometimes-tense differences among denominations, an unyielding, frequently hostile color line that kept black congregations from white ones, and signs of religion itself becoming a status symbol in the 1950s, religious faith seemed to Peale and other revivalists to unite the nation against an impersonal, godless enemy.

Peale had grown up in a highly devout home in rural Ohio. His father, a Methodist pastor, would tell locals persuaded to seek forgiveness, "I say to you that you are saved."[54] On Peale's graduation from Ohio Wesleyan University, where he had majored in English, his mother advised: "God wants you to serve Him. We have put you through college to qualify you to do great things."[55] After helping out in a Republican election campaign, during which he was offered "a stack of bills that 'would choke a cow,'" as one friend put it, seemingly for ballot stuffing, he took a job in Findlay, Ohio, as a reporter for the *Morning Republican*.

Ohio Wesleyan had banned smoking, drinking, and dancing before he enrolled. It was the start of Prohibition, for which Protestant churches expressed strong support, and the Peales were ardent campaigners in the effort to make Ohio "dry." As Carol George notes, "For evangelical Protestants like Clifford Peale," Norman's father, "the Prohibitionist movement became as much a religious as a social-political crusade." It came to stand for a "cultural struggle between native-born Protestant rural residents and immigrant, Roman Catholic, urban dwellers," who were perceived as heavier drinkers.[56]

Prohibition came into effect just as the Roaring Twenties began. The exuberance, at its height in wealthy pockets of the country, was partly in reaction to the temperance crusade. Then in October 1929, Wall Street's crash sent world markets haywire, toppling private enterprises and plunging America into the Great Depression.

In 1932, shortly before Prohibition ended, Peale accused "our Wet and vicious newspapers" of undermining it. By then a minister himself in Syracuse, New York, he called for the election of "an alternate set of Republican candidates" that would fight to preserve the abolition of liquor.[57] He somewhat later called for abstemiousness in a much larger sense when he warned about "sensuality," calling it a "supreme crime" and asserting that its pursuit led to a "decay of qualities."[58]

Given Peale's willingness to wade into a range of public and political controversies—from asserting that President Roosevelt showed an "indifference to religion" to questioning whether presidential candidate John F. Kennedy's Catholicism should not be opposed on political grounds—it is all the more striking that at college and during adolescence he suffered from brief but acute crises of confidence, especially when public speaking became necessary. At the same time, since he paired positive psychology with religious belief, he viewed such episodes as indicating a serious want of religious faith. The proposed solution: vigilance along with constantly renewed effort and commitment.

During religion classes that involved practice preaching, Peale would so dread his turn that he would fumble badly.

"I tried to emulate and copy" the most self-confident students, he writes in agonized remembrance, "but was all too conscious that I was pathetically inadequate." Such damning self-judgment would disappear during church services ("I forgot myself" then), but it would reassert itself implacably when he returned to his books and, in particular, when he tried addressing audiences off the cuff.[59] "My shyness made me tongue-tied and embarrassed when called upon to speak in public."[60]

Peale generally represented such behaviors as the result of "inferiority" and "inferiority feelings"—buzzwords that the psychologist Alfred Adler had recently popularized in reference to broken or collapsed self-esteem.[61] Such sentiments became both symptom and cause of Peale's "painful self-consciousness," since the awkwardness became self-fulfilling and resulted in a downward spiral of self-recrimination. "I grew red in the face," he writes of one particularly excruciating incident, and "nervously shifted from one foot to the other."[62]

Especially pronounced during adolescence, his shyness appears to have grown exponentially with his growing awe at his charismatic, larger-than-life father. The same pattern would recur with preachers, always male, who impressed the young Peale by speaking, as at the time he could not, with confidence and assurance. "I was fascinated by them," he wrote. "They had convictions, they were believers, and they were persuasive."[63]

Whereas Adler thought that perceived "inferiority" stemmed from mostly physical causes and could lead to a range of compensatory behaviors, Peale's father assumed that so-called inferiority came from guilt, largely of a religious kind. "Father described the mechanism of inferiority and self-doubt feelings in a manner that could do credit to a modern psychiatrist," Peale explained. "His perception that excessive guilt from bad thoughts, or wrong thinking about personality traits, could be harmful made him adept in dealing with my inferiority complex."[64]

This interpretation had the unfortunate consequence of turning shyness into a symptom of weakened belief. It made even fleeting signs of social awkwardness a barometer of religious faith and effort. For an evangelical Methodist, moreover, even a brief loss of faith was read less as doubtful wavering than as a heavenly rebuke for unworthiness. It amounted to a brutal withdrawal of God's love.[65] In short, the evangelical emphasis compounded guilt with assumed worthlessness, which made each recurrence of shyness harrowing, even tormenting. The problem built to a crisis:

> Finally Father asked me, "Norman, are you willing to let this great Doctor, Jesus Christ, treat you for that inferiority complex? If you let Him take charge of your mind, indeed your whole life, you can be freed of this misery which, if it continues, can destroy your effectiveness."[66]

The statement tells much about the way the younger Peale thought about—and later tried to combine—religion, psychology, and medicine. It makes religious conviction a precondition for mental *and* physical recovery. And although the medical health of non-Christians and nonbelievers might be thought a moot point, the distance of their problem from his own did little to persuade Peale that religion and perceived "inferiority" might have nothing in common.

As a younger man, Peale found that eager consent to have Christ "take charge of [his] mind" gave way to an immediate feeling of relief and euphoria; he could believe "I was really on top of my problems."[67] Yet when the shyness re-

turned, and it did several times—persisting, by Peale's reckon-
ing, as a minor problem throughout his life—it was treated
theologically, as an urgent need for a fresh commitment to
Christ.[68] During his first months of preaching in New York,
before he decided to open the Religio-Psychiatric Clinic, Peale
was beset by chronic self-doubt. His broadly professional
concerns—about the effectiveness of his sermons, among other
things—were interpreted, this time by his wife, as evidence
that he lacked religious conviction. "You just whine your defeat," she is reported as having complained. "And to put it
bluntly, what you need is a deep spiritual experience. You need
to be converted."[69]

Here is Peale's comment on the buildup to their argument:

> I was facing, in these depression times, my own
> minor depression in my new job at Marble Colle-
> giate. . . . I had a church that seated sixteen hun-
> dred people but had a congregation of only two
> hundred. Those empty pews haunted me. . . . So I
> preached sermon after sermon on faith, giving it
> other names like "belief in God" and then "belief in
> yourself," "belief in the future, your future." I called
> it the "power of positive thinking," unknowingly
> using a title later to be put on a book.[70]

The statement is revealing, both of Peale's self-adminis-
tered psychological solution ("belief in yourself") and of the
ease and need with which he combined belief in yourself with
"belief in God." It was as if, tellingly, the two had fused in his
mind and become interchangeable. The message of his sermons switched accordingly, from doom-laden, as in "Dr. Peale

Sees Freedom and Faith Periled," to positive, as in this summing up in his own words: "Trust God, have faith, stick it out, be a believer in the good heavenly Father, in your country, and in yourself."[71]

In the midst of the Great Depression, when many Americans were not just devastated financially but broken psychologically, his message hit the right note. Friendly advice to "have faith" and "stick it out" was balm to anxious, often destitute Americans fearful about their own futures but also that of their country. The broader question concerns the clinic's—and the foundation's—ambition to "encourage" patients, and Americans more generally, "to accept religiously motivated ideas and ideals as a means of solving personal problems."[72]

"If habits became ingrained through their repetition," Peale's father believed of a trait such as shyness, "then . . . by acting self-confidently, in time the pose would become the new habit, and the system would be purged of the old demon."[73]

The idea (strictly behaviorist) that one was being "purged of the old demon" got his emphasis exactly right, in that it turned his son's shyness into a trait both threatening to self and seemingly unworthy of God: it implied deficient faith in each. To prostrate oneself before God, helpless over its recurrence, then publicly to recommit to one's faith—was to release oneself from self-imposed strictures; it was to pair self-belief with religious piety until one or the other languished. After noting that Peale had sold aluminum pans to her just a few years earlier, one kindly observer of his early preaching encouraged him by saying: "I liked you, for you were young and confident and enthusiastic; and what a good salesman! Now you 'sell' the gospel with the same enthusiasm, if you don't mind my using that expression."[74]

In personal terms, joining religious enthusiasm to ardent self-belief did more than help Peale overcome his shyness. It gave him a way to "big himself up" and take on men as powerful as the president of the United States. By exuberantly proclaiming his faith, and to the largest number of witnesses, he could keep his supposed demons at bay while carving out a niche for his religious ambitions. Those, despite his insistence to the contrary, remained as fervently political as ever.[75]

As he put it to his local newspaper, far from bashfully or unambitiously: "Emotion breeds enthusiasm, and enthusiasm is that which is necessary to Christian world conquest. The great need of the church of today is a mystic or emotional contact with Christ. This will generate enthusiasm and vitality necessary for world conquest."[76]

IV

The Peale-Hoover-Eisenhower Empire

With "Christian world conquest" one of his stated goals, Peale looked for ways to attain it, first with devout, then with unchurched Americans. He urged pastors nationwide to embrace the use of radio, television, and film, warning that if the church failed to adapt and modernize, it would cease to be "an influential factor in American life."[1] What was needed, he felt, was a decisive push in the other direction. Religion should be so necessary and integral that the American way of life would seem unimaginable without it.

A message conveying a winning formula was crucial, Peale decided, and in his sermons, articles, and books he took pains to match religious faith with resounding health and success, to make the combination seem inevitable and self-reinforcing. In 1951, titles like "Formula for Efficiency" and "Science of a Satisfying Life" began to jostle with ones such as

"Faith Attitude Overcomes Every Difficulty" and "How to Be Reborn, or What Is Personal Resurrection?"[2] In *The Power of Positive Thinking*, his runaway best-seller published one year later, Peale opened by urging the reader to "Believe in Yourself! Have faith in your abilities!" He quickly turned to asserting, as in all his other writing, that faith should be religious in character. To maintain it, readers could try "prayer power," for which Peale was ready with a "formula" in attention-getting capitals: "(1) PRAYERIZE, (2) PICTURIZE, (3) ACTUALIZE."[3]

By turns pep talk, sermon, and sales pitch, Peale's book on positive thinking offered something of a mix, according to the theologian Reinhold Niebuhr: "a religion of self-assurance" and a "pious guide to personal success."[4] More persuasively than any other book from these years, it cemented for ordinary Americans a seemingly unbreakable connection between mental health and religiosity. At a time when Americans were encouraged to see themselves as living "under God," Peale insisted that they were also successful under God, their overall health and fast-spreading affluence a direct consequence of their religious commitment. Originally titled *The Power of Faith*—and retitled, according to Peale, after some personal reluctance—the book devotes a large portion of its pages to evangelizing.[5] Matthew 9:29 ("According to your faith be it unto you") was clearly one of Peale's favorite passages, for it repeats many times. "The greatest secret for eliminating the inferiority complex," Peale writes, again pairing positive psychology with religious conversion, "is to fill your mind to overflowing with faith." Not faith in yourself is meant here, but "a tremendous faith in God [as] that will give you a humble yet soundly realistic faith in yourself."[6]

A deficient faith implied an almost surefire risk of failure, as if all would be lost or taken in an instant. Citing as an authority an inspiring friend and fellow preacher who usefully surfaces at such moments in his books, Peale warns bluntly that "God will rate you according to the size of your prayers."[7] The judgment fails to surprise. The book makes almost fifty allusions to the Bible and almost as many to additional citations of its verses.

The "teach[ing] of faith" would vanquish "all manner of negativism," Peale assured, among which he classed religious doubt, poor health, and perceived inferiority.[8] In "Faith Attitude Overcomes Every Difficulty," a man diagnosed with rheumatic fever who has been wheelchair bound for twenty-seven years is told: "If you think in terms of defeat, it is because, may I respectfully suggest, you have been practising defeat for a long, long time."[9] The same faith would also strengthen America, Peale insisted, making religious devotion the sign of a robust and unified defense against communism and what Spiritual Mobilization, an organization on whose board he served, had taken to calling "pagan stateism."[10]

With religious belief cast as the means of transforming oneself, of restoring both mental and national health, positive thinking was made a vehicle for personal redemption and the best way to "effect a merger with God." This business-speak came from such earlier publishing sensations as *The Man Nobody Knows*, Bruce Barton's 1925 best-seller, which portrays Jesus as a successful business manager and Christians broadly as winners. A host of imitators followed, with advice on how to be God's Real Estate Man, God's Banker, God's Poultryman, and so on.[11] Peale's own book "surged to the number one position on best-seller lists all over the country," he recalls, after he appeared on Ralph Edwards's television show, *This Is Your Life*, one of the most popular at the time.[12]

By repeatedly equating business acumen with piety, uncertainty with religious doubt, and personal and cultural failure with godlessness, Peale and his admirers helped to redefine religious Americans as socially superior winners (the "better people," he once called them).[13] Almost inevitably, those without belief could be pictured as anxious, doubting losers, their unbelief as much a menace to the country as to the health of its citizens. Above all, self-affirmation was made a quality almost indistinguishable from religious faith. God was on America's side, encouraging the nation to yet greater heights.

Not surprisingly, questions began to be asked about the depth and seriousness of the "new piety." Of the trend that Peale was helping to intensify, the Reverend Harry C. Meserve noted in a 1955 article in *Atlantic Monthly*:

> The intensity of the struggle with communism in recent years has led many to believe that since communism is dogmatically atheistic in its philosophy, those who are opposed to communism must be dogmatically theistic. From here it is not a long step to the point where we make belief in God a test of a proper hatred of communism. And from this point one proceeds quickly to the assumption that God is not the Father of all mankind but the peculiar protector of the chosen people against the rest of the world. . . . We assume His sanction and aid for whatever we propose to do since He is on our side.[14]

Nevertheless, and doubtless partly because of the perceived exceptionalism, Peale's was a message that Americans were eager to hear and take to heart. For starters, it turned the Depression and the long years of austerity (predating more years of military conflict) into a test of religious faith and fortitude;

the affluence and piety of the fifties could then be coded, often quite explicitly, as a spiritual reward.[15] To Americans anxious about the nation's increasingly dangerous standoff with the Soviet Union and its allies, moreover, Peale's best-seller was a salve to anxiety and fear, promising a "gospel of reassurance and self-assurance."[16] By helping to turn religiosity into both a form of national defense and a self-help "vogue" or "fad," others complained, Peale's book made piety and mental health inseparable: a badge of success, patriotism, and personal status combined.[17]

By 1954, two years after publication, *The Power of Positive Thinking* had become a blockbuster. ("Actually," writes Peale in his autobiography, "it became 'one of the most successful books ever published,' to quote a researcher.")[18] The same year, he was named one of the country's Twelve Best Salesmen. His congregation was now at capacity; black and white photographs capture lines of expectant New Yorkers waiting to hear him preach. *Life* magazine reported that his church was "jammed twice every Sunday with 2,400 people, including many seated in two overflow chapels which carry the service on close[d]-circuit television. Hundreds are turned away."[19]

Either inaccurately or with invisible quotation marks around "discovery," the *Life* article claimed that "Doctor Peale's climb to public attention followed his discovery of the psychological basis of most individual disturbances." The article also offered a vivid description of Peale and his weekly activities, including his frenetic schedule and fierce motivation:

It would be easy to get the impression that Dr. Peale is more of an industry than a man. He's in his pulpit morning and evening on Sunday; he's on radio over

The Marble Collegiate Church in the 1950s with lines of people
waiting to enter. Courtesy the Peale History Center and Library,
Pawling, New York.

NBC from Monday to Friday and again on Sunday
before his church service; he (and his wife) are on
TV; his sermons are on records; his books are on
records; his magazine *Guideposts* is nudging the
800,000 circulation mark; he keeps one publishing
company going reprinting his sermons; he turns
out tons of "How to do" this and that cards, greet-
ing cards, Christmas cards; he estimates an average
of three speeches a week outside New York.[20]

To the list could be added the many books and articles he
wrote and the American Foundation of Religion and Psychia-

The Marble Collegiate congregation in the 1950s. Courtesy the
Peale History Center and Library, Pawling, New York.

try over which he presided. Within a few years, the Peale
Foundation for Christian Living—a sister organization over
which he also presided and the focus of his ministry—had
become, his biographer notes, "the clearinghouse for all Peale
activities and the center of what by [the mid-1950s] could only
be called an empire."[21]

That empire expanded rapidly across America, with both
the American Foundation of Religion and Psychiatry and the
Foundation for Christian Living tied to its financial benefits
and intended national effects; both aimed chiefly to evangelize
and equate mental health with religious belief. As one brochure for the former organization put it: "The American Foundation is bringing mental and emotional health to those who,

to some degree, have lost the zest of living. It restores their faith in themselves and in God."[22] The organization's emphasis on "religious healing" and "religiously motivated ideas" intensified what Peale took to calling "medicine's . . . necessary proclamation of faith."[23] One indicator of the reach of these organizations in the fifties is the mailing list of the Foundation for Christian Living, which grew from 50,000 to 325,000, mostly from interest in and publicity surrounding *The Power of Positive Thinking*. The building housing it "has been added to many times," Peale wrote in 1991, "and now contains more than seventy-five thousand square feet and employs 125 people, mailing Christian messages to a million people with a readership of 5 million." One of the mailings was *Guideposts*, which "has the twelfth largest circulation among all magazines published in the United States."[24]

One reason for Peale's now-vast following, the historian J. Ronald Oakley claims, was his careful "merging [of] religion, psychology, and the old American ideal of success." That combination of elements, which the American Foundation of Religion and Psychiatry would devote itself to fine-tuning and developing nationally, made it possible for Peale to win a huge audience and to "practic[e] mass counseling on an unprecedented scale through the means of modern communication." Oakley continues:

> In all of his books, sermons, records, and radio and television shows, he gave the same simple message over and over again: You can overcome any obstacle, have anything you want, obtain health, peace of mind, success, and popularity simply by believing in yourself, thinking positive thoughts, avoiding negative thoughts, convincing yourself that prob-

lems do not exist, using simple formulas, and taking God as a partner in life.[25]

Life also shrewdly tied Peale's popularity to his "rejection of
the dominant note of pessimism in the orthodox theology of
our time," noting his "ability to put that rejection in simple
rules."[26]

Still, as Peale's headline-grabbing sermons demonstrate,
there was another side to his sunny focus on "partnering with
God." Within a single paragraph, his prose could veer into ac-
cusation, especially over his reader's potentially poor motivation and still weaker faith regarding that partnership. "A most
pathetic mass of inner confusion . . . little short of mental filth"
is Peale's blunt assessment of one salesman's thinking.[27]

Personal transformation was in theory boundless ("The
rough is only mental," he liked to proclaim). Yet self-doubt
in Americans suggested to Peale—as it had to his father—a
worrying lapse of religious faith and mental health.[28] That assertion was now magnified a thousandfold across America by
Peale's phenomenal best-seller and his access to primetime
national media.[29] In 1957 he spelled it out distinctly: "Actually
it is an affront to God when you have a low opinion of yourself."[30] Failure of any kind had become anathema. "Never
entertain a failure thought," he warned, spotlighting the normally hidden underside to positive psychology. If you are
prone to such thinking, "you're disintegrating. You're deterio-
rating. You're dying on the vine."[31]

Mental-health experts and reviewers alike were far from persuaded. *The Power of Positive Thinking* took a "critical pummeling," one of Peale's biographers notes, in part for equating
negativity and failure with sin.[32] The book also relied on gener-

alizations and jargon that exasperated many. "The paragraphs could be shuffled and rearranged in any order," wrote William Lee Miller, then professor of religion at Smith College, in a withering review.

> As a result of reading Dr. Peale's [book], I am so full of "confidence-concepts," "faith-attitudes," and "energy-producing thoughts," of "thought-conditioners" and "spirit-lifters," of "10 simple, workable rules," "8 practical formulas," "7 simple steps," "2 fifteen-minute formulas," and a "3 point program," . . . of "healing words" ("tranquility," "serenity") and "magic words" . . . that I have the Confidence, Faith, Vigor, Belief, Energy, Efficiency, and Power to write an article criticizing Dr. Peale.[33]

Others faulted Peale for oversimplifying psychology, for rendering humanity both shallow and one-dimensional. "The mastery Peale speaks of," Donald Meyer cautioned from Harvard, "is not the mastery of skills or tasks, but the mastery of fleeing and avoiding one's own 'negative thoughts.'"[34] Similarly, Miller observed that Peale's advice amounted to "an optimism arranged by a very careful and very anxious selection of the particular bits and pieces of reality one is willing to acknowledge." The selectiveness, he added, spoke volumes about the present situation of the country, including—everywhere apparent and discussed—its religious sentiment and interest.[35]

Peale's reliance on autosuggestion was called unrealistic, "pollyannaish," and even dangerous, given its stress on the unproven and the unprovable.[36] The psychiatrist Robert C. Murphy complained that the book would shrink Americans' emotional range, since it shunned and rebuffed complex reactions, some of them an unavoidable part of being human. He commented bitingly:

> With saccharine terrorism, Mr. Peale refuses to allow his followers to hear, speak, or see any evil. For him real human suffering does not exist; there is no such thing as murderous rage, suicidal despair, cruelty, lust, greed, mass poverty, or illiteracy. All these things he would dismiss as relatively trivial mental processes [that] will evaporate if thoughts are simply turned into more cheerful channels. This attitude is so unpleasant it bears some search for its real meaning. It is clearly not a genuine denial of evil but rather a horror of it.[37]

Peale was also faulted on theological grounds, for tending to reduce God to human scale ("God is in you"), a position some denominations saw as quasi-sacrilegious and others as "syrupy" and as a false "cult of reassurance"—a 1950s religious version of "bright-siding."[38]

The pummeling did not end there. Critics complained that the book was "bursting with advertising," including for the Religio-Psychiatric Clinic, and that Peale's publishers had decided to market some editions by presenting them along with a free copy of the King James Bible. The leather-bound copies reached potential reviewers boxed together, "fastened with a brass clasp," and labeled "A Treasury of Faith." (This went "beyond vulgarity and presumption," wrote a *Saturday Review* contributor, "to the near reaches of blasphemy.")[39]

One way of viewing "the ferocity of the struggle between Peale and his opponents," Carol George notes astutely, is as an indication of "the magnitude of what was at stake for religion and the culture."[40] Part of that struggle took place around changing definitions of mental health and their relation to religious belief, with Peale's gospel of religio-psychiatry helping to make such elements seem inseparable.[41] Other signs of a shift in mindset, coordinated by evangelical groups like Spiritual Mobilization and the Christian Freedom Foundation, were the approval of such nation-changing acts as adding "In God We Trust" to the nation's currency after an intense, decades-long campaign. After 1954, owing to concerted effort by the Committee to Proclaim Liberty's "Freedom Under God" campaign, of which Peale was a major backer, U.S. citizens began to pledge allegiance to "one nation under God, indivisible." (No longer did they promise loyalty to the far more republican "one nation indivisible.") There was even an attempt the following year to pass a constitutional amendment asserting, "This nation devoutly recognizes the authority and law of Jesus Christ, Savior and Ruler of nations, through whom are bestowed the blessings of Almighty God."[42]

These were moves and signals for which Peale and other influential revivalists, such as Billy Graham, had spent years preparing. The two ministers collaborated in July 1957 on a "Crusade" to save New York City, after Graham staged a five-week religious revival in Washington, D.C., in January 1952 and held earlier high-profile "Crusades" in Atlanta, Fort Worth, and Los Angeles.[43] Those who supported the revival in Washington that year, Kevin Kruse notes, "were given cards to place in their Bibles, reminding them to pray daily "for the message of [the] Crusade to reach into every Government office, that many in Government will be won for Christ."[44] Such evangelical and political momentum, stretching in Peale's case back to the late 1930s, overrode the poor reviews of *The Power of Pos-*

itive Thinking—which in one sense gave it a larger spotlight and cast its author as embattled, a victim of elitist carping.

As earlier correspondence shows, the idea behind Peale's "Thought Conditioners" and *Spirit-Lifters* was not merely that autosuggestion would help Americans quell doubt and negativity; it was that the resulting "positive divine psychology"— their turning to God for reassurance—would have major cultural consequences by stimulating religiosity and identifying it with personal health and success.[45] "The homely, uncomplicated absolutes," Miller explained, seemed to offer "reassuring confirmation . . . that to men of simple faith all things are possible."[46] For Peale, any weakening of the national commitment to secularism would be a bonus.[47]

Peale's books and the clinic he founded with Blanton operated on the principle that the unconscious was a manifestation of God that needed careful, devoted release. In *Stay Alive All Your Life,* Peale offered a revisionary backward nod to Blanton's analysis with Freud: "There is resident in you an immense reservoir of force: the power of the subconscious mind. Faith releases this power."[48] Once on this footing, he could liken the unconscious to "soul" and claim that God—unlike the admonishing, often jealous deity of the Old Testament or the implacable superego portrayed by Freud in *Moses and Monotheism*— could be restyled as a kind, avuncular ally.

Far from advancing Freudianism, in short, Peale took the best insights he found and adapted them, turning the id as "cauldron" of primal aggression and home of the libido into a source of divine energy and heavenly illumination. The specifics did not appear to trouble him. As George notes, he "alternately identified personality, as in the Personality of Jesus, with Mind, soul, or subconscious as the motivating force for individual transformation . . . and the more he popularized his message, the fainter the original concepts became."[49]

Blanton maintained throughout his career-long affiliation with Peale that "man can never eliminate the aggressive origin of his energy" and that to hope otherwise was "a foolish fantasy which violates both scientific theory and common sense."[50] Peale claimed that faith could bend such properties, even guard what entered the unconscious in the first place. As he put it in *Faith Is the Answer,* clearly at variance with his co-author, "Religion teaches us to allow only good and beautiful thoughts to enter the unconscious because of the obvious fact often demonstrated that the unconscious can only send back what was first sent down."[51]

During their collaboration, Blanton encouraged Peale to read more of Freud, especially his last book, *An Outline of Psychoanalysis* (1940).[52] Years earlier, Freud had stipulated that psychoanalysis was "not satisfied with success produced by suggestion, but investigates the origin of and justification for the transference."[53] His caveat would seem to have major implications for the Religio-Psychiatric Clinic and the American Foundation of Religion and Psychiatry, especially the idea that "suggestion" was not a lasting way to alter thought, belief, or behavior. Far less directly, Freud's caveat could help explain why the intense religious sentiment of the fifties ran out of steam and even provoked a counterreaction.[54] Certainly, the presumed equation of mental health and religiosity was challenged.[55] Peale, however, was too taken with combining auto-suggestion and religious faith to view Blanton's advice as worthy of being heeded.

Whether on the road or zigzagging by train and sometimes private plane across the country, Peale did listen to one form of advice that turned out to be critical to his reaching nonreligious Americans. "You can't preach sermons to secular crowds," a consultant at a speaking agency warned him. "But having heard many of your sermons, I would say you could turn them into a speech."[56]

Signs of Peale's adopting the advice recur throughout his vast output, from "The Magic of Believing" and "Formula for Eliminating Worry" to "Are You Looking for God?"[57] When one audience member pipes up handily in the autobiography to assure everyone that Peale "could make a sermon out of that speech," the minister winks to the reader that he has in fact just done so.[58]

An anecdote in the autobiography helps convey just how seriously, and how personally, Peale took the effort to encourage and safeguard the nation's religious revival. In 1934, at an uptown New York meeting for "rising young businessmen," he describes asking the men on either side of him, without preliminaries, "Where do you go to church?" One answers hurriedly that he's a "nonactive Episcopalian," the other that his father and grandfather were Presbyterian. Neither reply satisfies Peale. The answer to his follow-up question, about how many Christians they would estimate are present at the meeting— "about 25 percent"—so disturbs the normally unflappable minister that he claims to need about forty blocks to walk it off. "Who are these guys," he fumes, "to look disparagingly on Christianity . . . ?"[59]

It is not clear from the autobiography that either man's words or estimate was disparaging. Indeed, they may have found Peale's opening question blunt, presumptuous, even accusatory. In the mid-1930s, for one in four attending such a meeting to be religiously devout is a conservative assessment, though by no means an insulting one. (Gallup data put Americans' weekly church attendance at the time at just under 40 percent.)[60]

If the business world sometimes disappointed, the political world was often more accommodating. One perhaps surprising ally—who was decisive in boosting the ambition of Peale and others for American religiosity—was J. Edgar Hoover, director of the F.B.I., who warned Americans about the perilous cultural "advance" of secularism and called the "godless tyranny of atheistic Communism" the nation's greatest threat.[61] Parents were "forgetting their God-given and patriotic obligations to the little ones," he warned in one of several invited contributions to Peale's *Guideposts: "Can a nation exist void of all religious thought and action?"*[62] Another ally was President Dwight D. Eisenhower, swept into office in 1953 after a landslide victory. In a nod to Peale, the president called religious faith his "shield" against fear and mental illness after Peale, moments earlier, had called him "God's chosen leader for this time of crisis."[63] The same president would tell the country that "recognition of the Supreme Being" was "the first—the most basic—expression of Americanism" and that "without God, there could be no American form of Government, nor an American way of life."[64]

Hoover and Peale corresponded throughout the religious revival, with Peale confiding in December 1956: "I cherish my friendship with you, for as you know, in my judgment, as well as in that of every American, you are one of the greatest leaders of our age, and will occupy an enviable place in the history of our country. God has called you to your position."[65]

They exchanged books, photographs, and material about the American Foundation of Religion and Psychiatry, whose progress Hoover noted with approval and pleasure.[66] Peale assured the F.B.I. director: "I feel a great sense of concern about the spread of Communism in this country, and want to do all I can toward strengthening the foundations of our freedom. If there is any time in which anything occurs to you that some of us can do to help support you in your work, I would appreciate knowing about it."[67] The correspondence extended to 1959, with Hoover thanking Peale for a flattering column in *Look* magazine: "The distinction you accorded me is most encouraging, and I am deeply appreciative of your generous comments. Yours is one of the finest compliments that it has been my privilege to receive, and I am humbled by the esteem you have placed in me."[68]

Eisenhower and Peale became sufficiently close for the minister, in one advertising brochure, to present the president as one of several high-profile admirers of *Guideposts* and *Spirit-Lifters* publications, as if the president were personally endorsing them ("satisfied customer").[69] Both men participated in the centerpiece of the "Back to God" movement, a "patriotic presentation" that aired nationally on multiple networks on February 1, 1953, in which Americans were urged to turn to prayer.[70] They also jointly addressed the 1957 F.B.I. graduating class, courtesy of its director, with the president reported nationally as declaring: "I am moved by the tenor of Dr. Peale's remarks . . . that there must be an underlying deeply felt religious faith if we are each to bear the burdens that are brought to our particular spot in our lives today. . . . I believe this thoroughly."[71]

Expressions of mutual admiration notwithstanding, Peale had fought ardently for the Republicans to nominate a quite different candidate. General Douglas MacArthur was at the time riding a wave of patriotic belief for leading the United States to military victory over the communists in northern Korea. "I doubt if you have any more loyal admirer in the

United States than the writer of this letter," Peale would later write the general.[72]

When Eisenhower won the election by a landslide, making inroads far into Democratic territory, conservatives such as Peale found it useful to throw their support behind him. But there are clear signs that the Republican leadership—noting the fervency of some of their party for MacArthur—tried to end the divisive primary by making religiosity the unifying issue. According to the Republican National Committee, the genial, fatherly Ike, as newly elected president, should be designated "not only the political leader, but the spiritual leader of our times."[73]

Eisenhower had previously attended church only sporadically, some noted in puzzlement, and did not belong to a particular church until after his election. Indeed, after the Reverend Edward L. R. Elson, minister to the capital's National Presbyterian Church, publicized rather too soon that Eisenhower would be attending his church, the president is said to have shouted at his press secretary, "You go and tell that goddam minister that if he gives out one more story about my religious faith I won't join his goddam church!"[74] The issue apparently concerned not religious commitment but the desire to appear nondenominational and thus religiously nonpartisan.[75] In his acceptance speech at the Republican convention, Eisenhower had asserted, right off the bat, "Ladies and gentlemen, you have summoned me . . . to lead a great crusade."[76] "Crusade" was a curious word to use, and so early in undertaking a political role, but one he would repeat three times in almost as many sentences. The billboards of his presidential campaign posed this question to citizens: "Faith in God and country; that's Eisenhower—how about you?"[77]

Taking a leaf from Peale and Blanton's *Faith Is the An-*

swer, the newly elected Ike took to generalizing that "faith is the mightiest force that man has at his command." His speech-writer opined in *Reader's Digest,* "What President Eisenhower wants for America is a revival of religious faith that will pro-duce a rededication to religious values and conduct." The pres-ident, the speechwriter conceded, had "one consuming ambi-tion: . . . to use his influence and his office to help make this period a spiritual turning point in America."[78] In *Piety along the Potomac,* Miller notes dryly: "One suspected at the time that the ghost-writer might be doing a little ghost-thinking. . . . It [was] at any rate a bit sudden. Mr. Eisenhower did not seem to be especially concerned with 'moral and spiritual' matters during his Army career." After coming into office, though, "crusades for this and crusades for that crisscrossed the coun-try . . . at a rate that must have been greater than the Holy Land ever knew, even in its busiest season."[79] Others began to hun-ger for a time when patriotism was not automatically religious in scope or effect.[80]

As president, Eisenhower began his inaugural address with a prayer and modeled his role as the nation's spiritual leader by opening each cabinet meeting with one. Not only did he make a point of being seen regularly attending church with his wife; he also made "frequent statements about the impor-tance of faith and the close ties between Christianity and Americanism."[81] Eisenhower expressed strong public support for "Operation Pray," sponsored by the Junior Chamber of Commerce in May 1953. His pastor opined, "It may not be too much to say that through his personal conduct and expression he has become, in a very real sense, the focal point of a moral resurgence and spiritual awakening of national proportions."[82]

Allusions to personal conduct can be risky. In 1954, Ei-senhower told the country to spend July Fourth as a day of prayer and penance; he, however, "went fishing in the morning, played 18 holes of golf in the afternoon, and bridge at night."[83] But in describing why he approved a congressional change to the nation's Pledge of Allegiance, the president truly tipped his hat:

> From this day forward, the millions of our school children will daily proclaim in every city and town, every village and rural school house, the dedication of our nation and our people to the Almighty. To anyone who truly loves America, nothing could be more inspiring than to contemplate this rededication of our youth, on each school morning, to our country's true meaning.[84]

So much "official religion in a land without an official religion" was becoming a distraction and a national problem, Miller complained at the time, not least in its "dubious mixture of patriotism and religion." Eisenhower had forged a relationship between his expression of faith and his role as president, crystallizing what would quickly amount to a constitutional problem for all Americans, especially those with no religious beliefs or with ties to other faiths.[85]

With politics and religio-psychiatry helping to drive the revival, Congress approved other legislation resulting in dramatic cultural changes that made America look and appear increasingly devout. And throughout the conservative fifties, much of the country embraced the message. "Year after year the statistics pointed to unprecedented increases in church membership," Oakley notes. It "grew from 86.8 million in 1950 to over 114 million in 1960. Each year saw record contributions to churches and other religious organizations, construction of new churches and synagogues and related religious buildings, record enrollments in college religion courses, overcrowding in religious seminaries, and growth in the prestige of clergymen."[86] Writing at the time, Miller, however, was more skeptical of the role of media and political figures in stoking the enthusiasm. In addition to Eisenhower, Peale, and other "chief leaders of this revival," he cited the stimulus of primetime media and mass communication in promoting the nation's religious turn. It was a time when newspapers not only reported the content of sermons by prominent ministers but also carried Bible stories in their feature and comic sections.

"There is a flood of so-called Biblical spectacles," Miller added, "with Hedy Lamarr as Delilah, Rita Hayworth as Salomé; and Cecil B. DeMille is busily parting the Red Sea and giving Moses a flaming love affair. These religious spectacles have, of course, been staple Hollywood fare throughout its history, but never in anything like the quantity of the present time." In 1953, he continued, "one out of ten books bought in the United States . . . was a religious book, whatever that may mean."[87]

Religious faith was being merchandised and sold to the American public as the must-have item of the decade, but also as the ticket to personal success and health. The newly ubiquitous and widely broadcast view of faith was transforming the nation and its mindset in ways that Peale's American Foundation of Religion and Psychiatry could only cheer and hope to strengthen.

V

Psychiatry Goes to Church

After Peale began marketing postcards encouraging prayer to "overcome an inferiority complex," a *Life* writer commented, "One wonders just what the clinic's psychiatrists with their top-flight medical training . . . think of their founder-president's preaching."[1]

Since the American Foundation of Religion and Psychiatry kept detailed records, such matters need not be conjectural. They shed light on its policies and practices, including its attempts to boost the nation's religiosity and adjust the country's understanding of the vexed, disputatious relations between religion and science.

Most of Peale's colleagues were delighted by the publicity he brought to the clinic and foundation, to say nothing of the funding and the sharp rise in patient interest. "Because of your ministry and your books," Blanton enthused to him privately in 1950, "as well as the work of the clinic itself, it [the clinic] has become known all over this country and Canada."[2] Claire Cox, the foundation's public relations director, saw her role as convincing clients and allies that "the most effective way of combatting the mental health problem of the nation is through religion and psychiatry" and that the foundation geared to address them was both "a missionary organization . . . and . . . an extension of the ministry of Norman Vincent Peale."[3]

What the combination of religion and psychiatry would yield, however, was often far from clear. While consensus remained strong inside the organization that it was managing to "combine the discipline of psychiatry with the profound influence of God," on the medical side of that equation, agreement inside the organization was much harder to find and developments were far from smooth.[4]

By 1955, four years after the American Foundation of Religion and Psychiatry had formally evolved out of the Religio-Psychiatric Clinic, Dr. Iago Galdston, its main intellectual advisor and the psychiatrist who had first put Peale and Blanton in touch with each other, wrote that he was no longer willing to be associated with either organization—that it would be best if he resigned. As he wrote Blanton, "I am frankly very unhappy about the 'tall talk' and slip-shod pretensions that are indulged in."[5]

Based at the prestigious New York Academy of Medicine and head of its Executive Committee on Medical Information, Galdston had also been serving as chair of the foundation's Committee on Research Studies, a position to which he brought status and credibility. He was, in the assessment of a key researcher, "responsible for turning the Foundation's attention in an academic direction"—one as interesting for the relations between religion and science as it would be for evangelicals and religious moderates on the question of health.[6] Yet, as Galdston noted delicately to Peale's assistant, "some of Dr. Peale's public pronouncements on issues of behavior and attitudes were not in accordance with the best thought in psychiatry." Given Peale's position as head of the foundation, it is reasonable (Galdston implied) to assume that outsiders viewed his claims as representative.[7]

The early concern that Galdston and other psychiatrists voiced about the way the Blanton-Peale clinic worked would recur, and forcefully. Several years later, in 1963, a staff member, Hugh S. Hostetler, the clinic's first full-time trainee, complained about the "absence of precise scientific and spiritual purposes" guiding the foundation's training programs. For example, clergy were advised to become counselors—a suggestion that had been circulating since at least the 1930s.[8] Hostetler shared his lengthy acrimonious letter of resignation with the entire board, including Peale. He claimed that in the absence of such guidelines, "the [Marble Collegiate] Church and its ordination" were being "illegitimately used as a front, masking pseudo-religious and pseudo-psychoanalytic rackets." He challenged the board: "Show me a student who has been strengthened religiously by his contact with the Foundation, and I will show you three cases of real damage done."[9]

Paul Hutchinson, who wrote the 1955 *Life* article, insisted, however, that "some people are helped." Even if the depression or anxiety of an individual was mild to begin with, "there are a lot of [patients], and if they can be helped before they fall prey to a serious neurosis, that is a service to society of no small value." The nation's rapid embrace of religiosity also drew Hutchinson's notice, not least because of Peale's work on many evangelical and political fronts. He called the result "a sort of alliance between one aspect of religion, the 'I will fear no evil' aspect, and depth psychology to overcome modern personality disintegrations."[10]

Still unparsed was the "profound influence of God" on

patients and whether or how that influence should combine with psychiatry. The members of the American Foundation of Religion and Psychiatry had little doubt that their organization had developed from "a remarkable clinic where doctors and clergymen join hands to mend broken souls and restore the shattered faith [of patients] in themselves and in God."[11] But beyond the foundation's ever-expanding targets of influence, as captured by its bullish annual reports and "extension activities reaching across the nation and around the world," whether religion and psychiatry *could* be "reconciled" was a fraught, potentially explosive issue.[12]

On the one hand, many psychiatrists viewed their discipline as necessarily secular—as neutral over religious beliefs and assumptions. To add piety to the mix might complicate diagnosis and treatment, confusing illness with sin and recovery with atonement. From such a standpoint, religion was too caught up in its own matters of judgment—in "accusing people of wrongdoing," in the words of one psychiatrist at the clinic—to advance its own best mechanisms for helping people in difficulty and need. On the other hand, the same psychiatrist continued, ministers "for a long time . . . have felt that psychiatry threatens their work."[13] The apparent neutrality over beliefs might also fail to reach the devout, for whom prayer would be integral and for whose relief of guilt and anxiety a spiritual authority would be necessary. Following the claims of Rabbi Joshua Loth Liebman in *Peace of Mind*, clinic staff noted that a minister could "be of tremendous help in motivating and giving permission for a patient to be ill and to seek help."[14]

Galdston was open to assessing religion's impact on health. As he noted to Peale's assistant, Howard LeSourd, in ways that recall Blanton's earlier discussions with Freud, a patient's trans-

Cover of the annual report of the American Foundation of Religion and Psychiatry, Winter 1965. Institutes of Religion and Health Records, Special Collections Research Center, Syracuse University Libraries.

ference could be considered integral to treatment, perhaps a placebo—an expectation of being cured, medically or religiously.[15] But it was, he thought, naive in the extreme to think that American psychiatry would come to view transference in general—and religious transference in particular—as the agent restoring mental health, especially in chronic cases.[16] For Galdston (unlike for Peale), assessing religion's *impact* on health was a proposition altogether different from binding religious belief *to* mental health, which made them seem coextensive and necessary to each other.

Peale tended to be unimpressed by such objections, even when they came from leading authorities in American medicine. As he privately fumed to Blanton in June 1955, concerning the objections of yet another critic:

> Incidentally, these men who spend their time working against me perhaps do not realize that I was invited to address the American Medical Association at its great convention in Atlantic City. I addressed six thousand doctors who packed the hall, and I think it is the first time any minister has ever addressed that organization. Also, I received an honorary degree (Doctor of Literature) recently from the Jefferson Medical College in Philadelphia, which is one of the half-dozen oldest medical colleges in the United States and the largest one. That is probably more than any of them have ever done.[17]

Regardless, building scientific credibility in the research program was paramount. Because "the foundation is a national institution," advised Samuel Klausner, a sociologist at

Columbia University who would publish exhaustive studies on religio-psychiatry, including its strengths, biases, and ideological assumptions, it "should have the kind of research which is proper for an institution in a movement of this kind." Key matters and sources of potential controversy were "the religious aspects of the Foundation in particular, in establishing policies combined with psychiatry."[18] Although Peale was still the foundation's principal source of financial support, Klausner pressed increasingly for its independence, which intensified concern about how the research would be funded while still assuring its national prominence.

The "best means of getting funds for the foundation," one financial advisor told its executive board frankly, "is to offer a service to corporations for which they could make a contribution or which they might call a 'retainer fee.'" One board member, Mrs. Arthur Kukner, added as bluntly to Peale and colleagues:

> I would like to make the following suggestions: Rexall Drug and General Motors to be the first two clients solicited on this, as the heads of these are already sold on the Foundation. We to offer to take care of 15 patients for General Motors and 10 patients for Rexall for the first six months or year in the clinic in return for a contribution of say $10,000 and $15,000 respectively. . . . We could easily, I am sure, manage 25 [patients] for these Corporations without increasing the staff.[19]

Across the top of his copy, Peale scribbled to his wife, then serving on the foundation's Development Committee, "Ruth, I think this is a top-notch idea," and urged a follow-up. Two years earlier, in 1954, the foundation had created a full-fledged "Corporation Committee" expressly designed "for solicitation of corporations."[20]

The foundation focused heavily on pharmaceuticals for treatment, hence perhaps the connection with Rexall Drug, Inc. At an October 1959 meeting, minutes record: "Mr. Tate spoke briefly on the use of drugs in the Clinic and the results obtained. He said by doing so it gave people a feeling of well-being with respect for themselves as well as others."[21] Though the statement lacks precision, it indicates that a foundation bent on combining psychiatry "with the profound influence of God" nursed perhaps surprising support for psychotropic medication.[22]

In the economic boom that followed the Second World War, during years that saw a sharp rise in national affluence and religiosity, middle-class Americans—housewives in particular— were annually consuming close to 1.2 million *pounds* of sedatives and tranquilizers like Miltown and Thorazine.[23] These were forerunners of the even more potent and addictive Valium and Librium, prescribed to millions of Americans in the 1960s and 1970s. Behind such numbers lay illnesses the American Psychiatric Association had included in its first and second editions of the *Diagnostic and Statistical Manual of Mental Disorders* (*DSM*), later dubbed the "bible" of the science. In the first edition, published in 1952, the thin, spiral-bound volume advised in the language and thinking of the time that illnesses could range from "Histrionic" and "Passive-Aggressive Personality Trait Disturbances" to those exhibiting "Emotionally Unstable" and merely "Inadequate" personalities.[24]

According to the 1952 *DSM*, persons with "Inadequate Personality" (000-x41) were "characterized by inadequate response to intellectual, emotional, social, and physical demands. They . . . show inadaptability, ineptness, poor judgment, lack of physical and emotional stamina, and social incompatibility." By contrast, a "Passive-Aggressive Personality" (000-x52) could exhibit such "trait disturbances" as "helplessness," "stubbornness, procrastination, and inefficiency"; characteristic behaviors included dallying over the laundry and shopping.[25] Although it is hard to believe that such descriptors were ever taken for science, the diagnoses were consequential. By 1966, "Passive-Aggressive Personality" helped account for more than 3 percent of hospitalized patients in U.S. public mental institutions and more than 9 percent of outpatients at psychiatric clinics.[26] Many other outpatients underwent electroshock treatment for depression and anxiety.

For its part, the American media gave the new "empire Psychotropia" almost giddy support, extolling the sedatives and tranquilizers with such descriptions as "Wonder Drug" (*Time*, 1954); "Happiness Pills" (*Newsweek*, 1956); "Aspirin for the Soul" (*Changing Times*, 1956); "Mental Laxatives" (*Nation*, 1956); "Don't-Give-A-Damn Pills" (*Time*, 1956); "Peace of Mind Drugs" (*Today's Health*, 1957); and "Turkish Bath in a Tablet" (*Reader's Digest*, 1962).[27]

In such an environment, the foundation's tacit support for pharmaceuticals may seem unremarkable. Yet it also sought drug-company sponsorship to investigate why "ministers and psychiatrists involved in the field of religion and mental health, and clients who seek their services, [were] a focus of opposition to the use of drugs in psychotherapy."[28] The research was meant to pair the use of pharmaceuticals with lower resistance to religious preaching and thus greater susceptibility to religious belief. The approach was designed to elicit financial patronage while keeping a focus on religious belief and its possible expansion nationally.

In a follow-up letter mailed to the research departments at an array of leading drugmakers, from Ciba, Merck, and Pfizer to Rexall, Warner-Lambert, and Wyeth, Blanton wrote of the use of pharmaceuticals:

> Ministers bring forth religious arguments against their use, clients report that they come to the religio-psychiatric clinic in order to avoid them, and even the medical people in this movement show hesitation in their application. We believe that in all of these cases the reasons for opposition to drugs go deeper than appears on the surface and merit some analysis.

Although Blanton did not elaborate on the reasons (among them surely the drugs' already well-established side effects), he added: "It has occurred to us that producers of pharmaceuticals would also be interested in this type of analysis. Our plan is to interview 750 ministers and psychiatrists in this field and 2400 clients."[29]

The strategy paid off handsomely. By November 1958, according to highly confidential foundation minutes, the Colgate-Palmolive Company had agreed to "offer the Foundation a half hour T.V. program daily (five days a week) with Dr. Peale interviewing a person, then turning the individual over to a panel of three members from the staff of the clinic." All of the panelists would discuss the case, then "solve" it, with Peale giving the closing statement. "For this service, the Colgate Company will pay the Foundation from $32,500 to $45,000 for a 13 week period."[30] The program—including the publicity and revenue it was expected to generate—was highlighted in subsequent fund-raisers for the foundation's research on "spiritual healing."[31]

By July 1966, the clinic had approved the establishment of a division on psychopharmacology aimed at determining still more clearly the loose but apparently suggestive combination of psychiatric counseling, pharmaceuticals, and religious belief. It was the task of the division to "evaluate clients for medication and see that there is no danger involved."[32]

In presiding over a foundation to which he continued to assign a generous portion of his royalties, Peale drew repeatedly on his own ministry and business connections, soliciting "support from churches, industry, [and] other community sources to whom an affiliate could give support."[33] In return, as the executive director noted, an affiliate of the foundation could count on "the extension of [its] 'know-how' to every strategic care-taking group in the community, particularly the teacher, the family physician, the industrial nurse, the police, etc." Furthermore, "the same techniques and methods that have been applied to the training of clergy can be applied to these other groups."[34]

Although such "know-how" and "techniques" remained nebulous, as even insiders complained, they were understood to include "spiritual healing" and the "encourage[ment of patients] to accept religiously motivated ideas and ideals as a means of solving personal problems."[35] "The religious factor" would also play a role in the foundation's research, in the "prevention and early detection of mental illness"—although how and to what degree was never determined.[36]

In 1964 the foundation's executive director, Arthur

Tingue, circulated for approval a "Program to Relate the Work of the Foundation to the Needs of Executives and Corporations." It stated: "Employees feel that they can trust a clergyman with confidential information. . . . The foundation can provide expert pastoral counseling to help employees handling their personal problems and thus become more productive members of their companies." Adopted enthusiastically, the proposal was designed to create a "concrete program to serve executives and industry." Once ready, it could be announced in "a major address to the World Federation of Mental Health, and through local newspaper articles."[37]

Among the same packet of proposals was a plan to extend the foundation's reach across the nation—beyond the affiliates already established in the Midwest and California, with subsidiaries now pending in Seattle, San Diego, Houston, Dallas, Boston, Philadelphia, and Providence.[38] The proposal, titled "A Program to Relate the Work of the Foundation to the Needs of National Religious Leaders," was designed "to foster theological thinking" across the United States. It was tailored to reach "every phase of the religious community of the nation," not to mention J. Edgar Hoover and President Eisenhower.[39]

With Peale fervent in his desire for the mass counseling of Americans through religion and psychiatry and Blanton fascinated by the tenacity of religious transference in cases such as that of Charles McDonald (the Dubliner with tuberculosis who had visited Lourdes), the foundation put enormous weight on "spiritual healing" and the need to study its effects. The clear, often-expressed wish was that "spiritual healing" would be given unassailable bona fides. That would make the coupling of psychiatry and religion seem both natural and inevitable.

The effort drove hours of discussion, generating sheaves

of documents. As Samuel Klausner summed up from just a few of the meetings he had been invited to attend: "Questions were posed. Could research evaluate cooperation between ministers and psychiatrists? Were people cured through church healing services? Could the power of prayer be measured?"[40]

But the focus on verifying "spiritual healing" also generated friction between Blanton and Galdston, accelerating the latter's departure. As Klausner noted dryly:

> Dr. Blanton invited Dr. [E. Baylis] Ash, a member of the Royal Medical Society [in London] who had relinquished his medical practice to devote himself to faith healing, to lecture at the Clinic. Dr. Ash described a force coming out of his finger-tips which when held over a patient's infected leg caused the infection to recede. From California Dr. Blanton brought Dr. William R. Parker, who subsequently wrote *Prayer Can Change Your Life—The Scientific Proof That Prayer Can Bring You What You Want.* When Dr. Parker, a Professor of Speech at Redlands University, found himself on the verge of a nervous breakdown, he began to pray and in a few months was entirely well.[41]

The assertions presented conclusions too hasty and scattershot to support the religious claims that Peale and Blanton so longed to attach to them. What was tantalizing to Blanton was, in short, almost useless to Galdston:

> Dr. Parker set up counseling groups. One group received traditional group psychotherapy. A second group prayed generally for therapy. A third group

used prayers specifically related to their difficulties. Dr. Parker reported that members of the third
group showed most improvement.[42]

Before resigning, Galdston "insisted that an outside
agency be called in to do the research." He recommended the
Bureau of Applied Social Research at Columbia University,
where Klausner was then working.[43] Galdston's departure
shortly thereafter led to no shift in direction at the foundation.
On the contrary, the wish for medical and scientific recognition of "spiritual healing" burgeoned into something of an ob-
session, with tempers flaring. Patience was stretched so far
that Peale would eventually fire off a letter to the president of
Columbia University, soliciting his personal assurance that research the foundation had paid for would at last be completed.

Although the tense exchange between an Ivy League president and one of the nation's most prominent ministers cannot
have done much to ease the pressure, Klausner, the diligent,
low-key researcher caught in the middle, ran into difficulties
shortly after Galdston left. His project—ambitious but loosely
defined—soon spiraled off in so many directions that it became unworkable. The foundation wanted him to study the
state of affairs between ministers and psychiatrists, the client
population at the clinic, and the nature and effectiveness of
religio-psychiatric therapy overall. But to measure the therapy
overall with any claim to credibility, Klausner needed a reli-
able definition of "faith" as the foundation and its patients understood the term. That meant developing a scale by which to
gauge its impact on treatment.[44]

Other desired areas of investigation, such as the "validity
of 'cures,'" were, his boss at the Bureau of Applied Social Re-

search insisted warily, "questions . . . we do not feel equipped to handle."[45] Funds to complete approved stages of the research kept running dry. With the clinic itself upheld as the object to be studied, exemplary of religio-psychiatry as a whole, there was also the delicate question of whether those sponsoring the research would accept results that might be unfavorable, even unflattering.

The Peale and Blanton expectations were doubtless too high. Shortly after his arrival at the foundation, Klausner noted ruefully that "ministers and psychiatrists hoped a researcher would help them verbalize what they were doing." A few staff members, he noted, also "wondered whether the researcher would be reporting their behavior to Drs. Blanton and Peale."[46]

The proposals on "spiritual healing" began with suppositions that often begged the central question. One claim maintained, without example or clarification, that "some neuroses have specifically religious as well as psychological aspects and that effective handling of such cases requires the cooperation of the psychiatrist and the minister."[47] The bureau was better equipped and more willing to ask, with scrupulous quotation marks, "What is the culture of 'faith healing'? How does it compare with magic and witchcraft in primitive cultures? What is the nature of the relationship between the leaders and the led? What is the relation between a 'cure' and ideas, beliefs or values?"[48]

In the book that eventually appeared, fully eight years after the start of the research and after a volley of letters, Klausner credited colleagues at the bureau for "help[ing] me maintain a sociological perspective on the topic."[49] Relations between foundation and bureau had long since soured. Months before publication, concern was voiced internally at the foundation that the book "does not accurately depict the work of the foundation at the present time."[50] For his part, Klausner went on to concede to Blanton that "the first error was to divert energy from work on the single minister-psychiatrist project to take up research on faith healing. . . . The second poor decision was to assume that our relationship was a long-range one, that we were sort of a permanent research department of the foundation."[51]

Although Blanton and Peale clearly hoped that the bureau would give "spiritual healing" enough credibility to declare it scientifically plausible, Klausner was far more interested in the alliance between ministers and psychiatrists—an alliance that sprang from the very revival the foundation had promoted, from which it also drew strength. What had helped bring the ministers and psychiatrists together, he determined, was a sense of "alienation" from their primary groups, which they had tended to find rigid and doctrinaire.

Klausner found that when ministers suspended preaching to focus on the pastoral side of their work, they invariably joined psychiatrists in wanting to reduce the suffering of their patients. Yet there were telling differences in expectations and approach. "One function of the psychiatrist," a staff member at the clinic declared in a recorded interview, "is to remove unconscious barriers to a normal religious life. I have a man whose father is a devout orthodox Jew. This boy thinks religion is bunk. I can help him to realize that his attitude toward religion is a reaction to his resentment toward his father."[52]

Nor were the ministers practiced in putting aside their religious values—or in imagining that they ever needed to. In response to a question as to "whether a homosexual must assume an obligation to cooperate and change," one minister in another taped interview thundered: "The Lord will not accept a sinner who does not intend to correct his sin." Another said,

"Homosexuality is against the tenets of religion; it is one of the sicknesses of the human race."[53]

As the *DSM* diagnoses on "histrionic" and "inadequate" personalities underline, American psychiatry was far from neutral on such matters. Until 1973, it classified homosexuality as a mental illness and had strenuously opposed earlier efforts to remove it from the manual. The American Psychiatric Association agreed to a change only after months of rancorous debate. The agreement was to substitute fresh diagnoses—first, "sexual orientation disturbance," then "ego-dystonic homosexuality," and then "gender identity disorder."[54]

Perhaps mindful that he had taken on an increasingly beset and never-ending project, with conclusions certain to dissatisfy his sponsors, Klausner took to cataloguing the religious background of the authors he had unearthed along with a host of other empirical factors, yielding a trove of data. Scientific measurement of whether prayer accelerated medical recovery, and if so how rapidly, was quietly dropped from his to-do list.

Klausner's research eventually could confirm that the ratio of ministers to psychiatrists in the United States was "very high . . . about 40:1."[55] He assembled graphs and tables showing that by 1963 the religio-psychiatry movement that had shown such vigor and evangelical dedication in the 1950s had begun to "mellow." By this he meant that it had become less strident, more ecumenical, and—significantly—more willing to substitute a "spiritual" for a "religious" focus.[56] Although the foundation indeed grew less evangelical over time and more interested in the possibilities of nonsectarian interfaith, an emphasis that has continued,[57] Klausner nonetheless found that the movement as a whole "was becoming more homogenously Protestant." It was also, he ascertained, becoming less successful at integrating differences between faiths, even as it "function[ed] as one of the principal platforms for the encounter between religion and science."[58]

Among the broad trends in the United States, Klausner could determine that between 1948 and 1957 the number of publications on religio-psychiatry had almost quadrupled over the number in the previous decade and had risen thirteenfold since the 1920s. From interviews with psychiatrists and ministers, he devised a "religious belief index" and a "psychiatric belief index," offering valuable snapshots of the thinking over time.[59]

According to his psychiatric index, fully half the 478 *ministers* interviewed affirmed that "the good is achieved through science. Even religion is a function of science and may be judged by science." Equally significant, almost half (44 percent) of the 140 *psychiatrists* agreed with the statement "I believe in a general moral force or God as expressed in man's relations or God as a symbolic archetype." Only 11 percent of the psychiatrists held to the conviction that "there is no personal creator. The world is governed by natural laws."[60]

Klausner's focus on *religio*-psychiatry greatly increased the odds that the psychiatrists in his sample would be devout. From his survey of the literature, however, he could show that a convergence between psychiatry and religion was taking place nationally; both had moved in from the polar extremes they had assumed just a decade earlier. Although other conclusions also mattered (including conclusions about "spiritual healing"), he showed that the Peale-Blanton gospel of "religio-psychiatry" had helped to narrow the divide between religion and "science," at least as Peale and Blanton used the last term.

Klausner's book opens with real-life vignettes whose theme is frustration over the "war" between science and religion:

> A Protestant minister in New York leaves his pul-
> pit to become a full-time psychological counselor.
> A church dignitary accuses him of perverting his
> ministry. In Barcelona, a Catholic psychiatrist helps
> patients find a new relationship with God. His col-
> leagues attack him for scientific irresponsibility.
> The minister and the psychiatrist discover one an-
> other and make a common cause. Thus, a psycho-
> logical ministry and religious psychiatry create an
> unorthodox alliance to battle personal misery. The
> religio-psychiatric movement is born through sev-
> eral thousand similar encounters.[61]

Like the book's opening, with its distant, adjusted allusion to Peale and Blanton, Klausner's conclusions about a future "pathway between religion and science" were cautious and for the most part unsurprising.[62] Still, the convergence he documented could be seen taking place in many similar quarters. Articles in popular forums carried titles such as "Psychiatry Goes to Church"; among academics, interest lay in "The Common Grounds between Psychiatry and Religion."[63] With the president of the American Medical Association, Peale published a brochure called *Medicine's Proclamation of Faith*, which focused once more on the "role of faith" at the clinic. This time it called all the doctors of America "servants of God."[64]

There were further signs that the antagonism between religion and science was softening, even moving strongly in religion's favor. The Group for the Advancement of Psychiatry published two reports on psychiatry and religion, urging greater consilience and respect for patients' religious beliefs.[65] The American Medical Association and the American Psychiatric Association each created organizational divisions of religion and health. A group of clinical psychologists in the American Psychological Association also began sponsoring sessions at its annual convention.

Yet the undertow of evangelism had not entirely disappeared, so the implications of the convergence were not always clear. The results became especially hazy when leading figures in the field used their platform and opportunity to evangelize, as Karl Menninger did when he declared: "The basis of all religion is the duty to love God and offer our help to His children—and psychiatry, too, is dedicated to the latter duty."[66]

Peale clearly found Klausner's thoroughness and push for neutrality exasperating; he wanted speedy answers that he could showcase in foundation brochures, to signal (as its executive director put it) that the foundation was "ready to move with the space age."[67] After umpteen delays and renegotiations, he fired off a letter to the president of Columbia University, then Grayson Kirk, complaining: "We have invested approximately $75,000 in this work, and I am sorry to say that up to the present time we have very little in concrete form to show for it."[68]

Promised since December 1959, Klausner's book was at that point two years late. "It may indeed be some time before the book itself is published," bureau staff advised weakly.[69] Peale insisted to Kirk that they had been "most patient" but that the delay had become a source of "considerable embarrassment."[70]

Columbia's president bristled at the implication that the bureau had been slack in carrying out its work and called Peale's phrase "very little in concrete form to show for it" a "serious charge." He advised Peale that Klausner had in fact produced twenty-three unpublished reports on the topic and six scholarly articles, following two hundred days of consultation. While Kirk too hoped for the project's timely completion, he cautioned that rapid publication was "somewhat unrealistic" and that inferior work due to haste would be a disappointment to all.[71]

Among other things, the episode shows how strongly Peale needed religio-psychiatry to be taken seriously, how hard the foundation fought to give "spiritual healing" academic credibility, and how the convergence between religion and science raised fresh, somewhat urgent questions about the terms on which they were merging. Although Klausner and the bureau were unable to establish scientific proof of the value of the convergence, at least in the form wanted, the foundation pressed on, looking for ways to expand nationally even as signs mounted that the religious revival was flagging.[72] It appointed a U.S. senator to its executive board (W. Russell Arrington, R-Illinois); attended a White House initiative on mental health led by Lyndon B. Johnson; strove for influence in countries as far afield as India, Australia, and New Zealand; and ultimately replaced Peale as president with W. Clement Stone, the positive-thinking guru and evangelist who had made his fortune selling insurance.[73]

Stone chaired the foundation's board from 1962 until 1973, extending Peale's business-friendly approach, along with his emphasis on prayer and the need for a "Positive Mental Attitude" (PMA). He also increased the gift-giving program for donors, this time in the realm of millions. One report detailing plans for global expansion—through alumni initiatives abroad—boasted that the impetus was "based on the principle expressed by Mr. Stone when he wrote, 'You can motivate an-

other person to do what you want when you give him an opportunity to get what he wants.'"[74]

Like Peale, Stone thought that the unconscious could be
altered by verbal repetition. He wanted Americans to think
and act on a grand and generous scale. He was himself one
of the largest financial contributors to the election campaigns
of Richard M. Nixon. The writer of the *New York Times* obituary in 2002 felt obliged to note that "Mr. Stone's contributions
of more than $2 million to President Nixon's re-election cam-
paign in 1972—on top of even greater donations to Mr. Nixon
in 1968—were cited in Congressional debates after Watergate
as a reason for instituting campaign spending limits."[75]

Such close political ties while Stone was alive may explain why sister organizations such as the Academy of Religion and Mental Health, were by March 1965 actively and
"constant[ly] denigrating" the American Foundation of Religion and Psychiatry.[76] The alliance between psychiatry and religion had reached a point of complex negotiation where any
impulse to evangelize could lead it to founder. Relations with
science would improve only if organizations became more religiously moderate and gave up equating health with religious
conversion. Since Stone was then president, the reproach came
on his watch. By the mid-1960s, however, the foundation was
practiced in fending off criticism and spinning its past. It focused on blending science with religion to avoid detailing the
rougher edges of its evangelical history. Claire Cox, the foundation's public relations director, urged her colleagues to "dra-
matize and romance the story of the American Foundation . . .
to help in the promotion of [its] national and international
development program."[77]

A feature since its inception, the foundation's impulse to

evangelize—to promote "prayer-power" and "save" both individuals and the nation—had dimmed but far from disappeared. While the effort to cement mental health and religious belief had receded more or less conclusively, the accumulated effects of that effort would be felt far into the future, with scholars and researchers needing decades to unpick them. Even so, evangelicals and religious conservatives would continue to push for new ways to align piety with health, sometimes by rejecting science altogether.

VI

Religion and Mental Health Rebalanced

In the opening issue of the 1960s, *Harper's Magazine* lost no time declaring "goodbye to the 'fifties—and good riddance." The Princeton historian Eric F. Goldman, who wrote the keynote article, placed the blame squarely on the religious revival: "We live in a heavy, humorless, sanctimonious, stultifying atmosphere. . . . Over the whole of this land, a kind of creeping piety, a false piety and religiosity . . . has slithered its way to astounding popularity."[1]

The magazine article was designed to startle and provoke; the frustration with Peale-like positive thinking was everywhere apparent. In a sign of the wide-eyed enthusiasm that Goldman hoped to end, he quoted the high-profile broadcaster Arthur Godfrey as urging: "Don't tell me about science and its exact explanation of everything. Some things are bigger. God is the difference. He gets around."[2]

"Don't tell me about science." With Peale, not to mention

other evangelicals, arguing that "religion may be said to form an exact science" and that religion and psychiatry could coexist quite happily, his many followers and admirers might think that problems identified by science were somehow already answered and explained.[3]

Like other critics of the revival, including those concerned about the notion and effects of "government under God," Goldman wanted the whole edifice of "false piety and religiosity" dismantled, as if its now-widespread effects could best be countered by satire and mockery. "The ground must be cleared of confusing and distracting carry-overs from the past," he wrote, "even from the immediate past." Customs, traditions, and beliefs—if in any way backward-looking or irrational— needed to be swept away so that an "overfed, oversanctified" nation could focus on the challenges of a scientific age.[4]

On the relations between science and religion, other commentators were less extreme, recognizing that Americans' religious beliefs were disparate, resilient, and likely only to harden in response to scorn. "Fully two-thirds of the adults in our country regard themselves as religious people," the Harvard psychologist Gordon W. Allport reported midcentury, "and at least nine-tenths, by their own [account], believe in God."[5] At the time, ninety-three million Americans identified themselves as members of religious organizations.[6] Even (or especially) with the revival fading among so-called mainline Protestants, Catholics, and Jews, evangelical conservatives continued to find considerable political support in the administration of Richard M. Nixon—and, in the coming decades, in those of Ronald Reagan and George W. Bush. Thus, an open call for satire and mockery seemed unlikely to narrow the still-yawning chasm between the country's scientific followers and its religious communities.[7]

To many of the latter group, "Science Isn't God," the headline of a Southern newspaper in the early 1960s, rang true. It invoked fallibility and metaphysical authority, to say nothing of the stresses of the space age.[8] That science—in particular, psychiatry—had its own controversies and blind spots, even as it sought to investigate them, drove such questions in the editorial as "Is it possible, as has been proposed, that a new science could be created to keep society from committing suicide with nuclear weapons? Can a science of human survival be developed, or is one necessary?"[9]

To restore dialogue and encourage less polarized positions, organizations such as the Institute on Religion in an Age of Science conceded in 1963 that "the impact of modern science upon religion is as revolutionary as the impact of modern technology upon our everyday life."[10] With growing national concern about nuclear energy and weaponry (the Cuban missile crisis had taken the world to the brink for thirteen terrifying days the previous October), the institute advised at a conference that participants and Americans at large be open-eyed and unafraid. "Neither science nor religion alone can guarantee human welfare; only when there is wise integration of the knowledge and aspirations of both can there be any real hope for mankind, individually and collectively."[11]

The desire for convergence between religion and science—including, most centrally, between religion and psychiatry—was a common theme of books and articles of this era. Many of them pressed for subtler, more measured efforts to integrate the two, in ways that would avoid the reductive traits of Peale's religio-psychiatry. There was a strong emphasis on shared concerns, among them the growing number of Americans diagnosed as mentally ill and the need to provide them with adequate care. As Allport put it eloquently, "Our common aim is to fortify the human spirit so that it can withdraw from the brink and to help those who have fallen to regain their footing."[12]

Much of the ensuing adjustment, evidence suggests, came from religious moderates keen for rapprochement with the scientific community and increasingly critical of the rejection of science by their evangelical counterparts. "Since we cannot and will not turn our backs on the modern world," Allport wrote earnestly, "the religion we embrace cannot be pre-scientific; nor anti-scientific; it must be co-scientific."[13] For their part, many scientists, as organizers of a "Religion, Science and Mental Health" symposium in 1957 noted with approval, had expanded their range of interests to include "entire areas of human behavior that were formerly considered outside the province of their study."[14]

The 1950s religious boom continued to fade over the next decade, in part from cracks appearing between religious traditionalists and their chosen representatives. These included stark differences over the June 1962 Supreme Court ruling about prayer and government (*Engel v. Vitale*): that creating an official state prayer and encouraging its repetition in public schools was unconstitutional. Religious observance dropped sharply among mainline Protestants, with smaller though significant recorded falls among Catholics and Jews.[15] Public expressions of piety, of the kind broadcast by Eisenhower at the height of the religious revival and summed up by the slogan "Government Under God," had lost much of their luster. Even with the nation bogged down militarily in Vietnam and President Kennedy shockingly assassinated in November 1963, the broader turn was not toward religion, as might have been expected, given recent precedent, but away from it. The number of Americans who believed that "religion can answer today's problems" dropped sharply, from 81 percent in 1957 to 62 percent in 1974. Church attendance fell seven percentage points across a similar interval, plummeting to 42 percent by 1969.[16] In April 1966 an infamous cover of *Time* magazine read, "Is God Dead?" Two scholars summed up the country's dramatic transformation: "Almost overnight, it seemed, America had turned from God's country to a godless one."[17]

Despite Clement Stone's ambitious plans for the continued expansion of the American Foundation of Religion and Psychiatry, it was by the late 1960s experiencing a loss of direction and support. Peale had stepped down as president in 1962, and Blanton died four years later. According to a summary attached to the November 12, 1968, minutes, "The administrative and development activities of the Foundation did not continue to merit the confidence of the members of the Boards. Many of these people were serving because they had been helped through the clinic or because they had a feeling of loyalty to Dr. Peale, Dr. Blanton or Mr. Stone. They began to feel uninformed and uninvolved."[18]

Attempting to retain some its influence from the previous decade even while solving the $3.8 million shortfall in its annual budget, the foundation voted to join its more secular counterpart, the Academy of Religion and Mental Health, creating from the merger the Institutes of Religion and Health. Partly because of their earlier differences, the merger would end after three years, with only a much-altered version of the Religio-Psychiatric Clinic intact. The push for the merger was indicative of adjustments across the country, even as questions about the evangelical premises of Peale's religio-psychiatry remained. In striving to promote a more global interfaith dialogue, ostensibly the American Foundation of Religion and Psychiatry would cease to evangelize through psychiatric counseling. Before the merger, foundation board members were nonetheless reassured: "The Academy believes that the ethical, spiritual, and moral values of the individual play a major role in determining his reaction to stress. Because of this, religion must be orchestrated into psychotherapeutic methodology as an important adjunct to medicine and psychiatry."[19] The devil of the "orchestration" would lie in its details.

Founded three years later than Peale's American Foundation for Religion and Psychiatry, the Academy of Religion and Mental Health was created in 1954 as "a nonprofit, non-sectarian membership organization" aimed at restoring dialogue between religion and science, chiefly through academic channels.[20] By 1965, with pilot training programs under way at Harvard, Yeshiva, and Loyola Chicago Universities (funded by the government's National Institute of Mental Health), after some twenty-five hundred discussion meetings between psychiatrists and clergy, the academy assumed a leadership role in "scores of other projects and activities" both nationally and internationally. According to Kenneth E. Appel, then chair of psychiatry at the University of Pennsylvania, its membership came to include "many of the most distinguished physicians, behavioral scientists, and theologians in the world."[21]

Unlike Peale's foundation, which had always been more focused on marshaling and converting the American public than in persuading the nation's scholars, the academy recognized that relations between religion and psychiatry were complex, historically tense, and unstable. Any change would have profound cultural and philosophical implications, not least for a nation recently caught up in a wave of religious and patriotic feeling.

Early in 1954, George Christian Anderson, an Episcopal

clergyman studying abnormal psychology at Columbia, had written and circulated a brief statement he called "Comprehensive Man." He proposed that as "man is more than a mere biological entity, . . . there is need for accord between what has been called scientific medicine and what is termed comprehensive medicine." Finding and cementing that accord would prove far from easy.[22]

Among the chief reasons for Anderson's own difficulty was a clear personal reluctance to put science and religion on an equal footing. More or less from the outset, the reverend let the balance tilt in religion's favor. He asserted without explanation or evidence: "Until some sort of working agreement can be reached concerning basic motivations and purposes behind human existence, the logical and reasonable conclusions of science need to be examined in the light of intelligent theological attitudes."[23]

Did the statement include Freud's and Darwin's findings, even—potentially—those as far back as Galileo's? Anderson did not elaborate, although history was plainly important to him. "The words 'health,' 'whole,' 'holiness' come from an old English word, 'hal,' meaning complete," he noted, signaling the roots of his thinking as at least premodern. The connection led him to infer that health must "involve harmony of body and mind, which implies integration with oneself, one's neighbor, and one's cosmos." Mental health seemed to require a connection to the universe, although Anderson was sketchy about the details. "Man is not only a human being in a social environment," he contended; "he is also related to eternal values."[24]

From such a claim, hazy though it was, the Academy of Religion and Mental Health moved to support an even older religious argument that emotional or mental illness was in fact "soul sickness," calling for some form of theological rebuke. As Anderson declared in the academy's founding document: "Mental health from a religious viewpoint involves not only harmonious relations between man and his God, but between man and society."[25] By implication, the absence of mental health implied an element of religious friction or adverse judgment.

In, for instance, "Health from the Standpoint of the Christian Faith," an essay from the height of the religious revival that Anderson quoted approvingly, the author asserted matter-of-factly:

> Neurotic conflict results in (a) self-estrangement, (b) estrangement from other human beings, and (c) estrangement from God or the ground of creativity (however conceived); and these are so functionally interrelated that it is impossible to divorce one from the others.[26]

No true mental health was apparently possible without an end to "estrangement," whatever that implied or seemingly required. Unlike the foundation, whose efforts throughout its existence had been to proselytize, to help promote the revival of faith, and to solder belief in self to belief in God, Anderson was quick to recognize that "religious experiences do not always lead to mental health"; they "may aggravate mental illness" and "become factors in a neurotic development."[27] Much depended on the type and intensity of religiosity experienced—whether a person's beliefs bordered on fanaticism or amounted to "mature belief," as Allport put it—belief of the kind that "grows painfully out of the alternating doubts and affirmations that characterize productive thinking."[28]

Just as critical, Allport and the academy found, was

whether someone's seeming internal religious direction was harsh and condemning or benign and self-supportive. Whether individuals could "satisfy" and "live up to" the ideals and goals set by their faiths was similarly understood to have a profound bearing on their level of happiness or anxiety.[29] "Some religious motivations"—here, zeal and fanaticism were implied—"tend to intensify the neurotic conflict." There were, in short, "neurotic and healthy uses of religious belief," just as there were "healthy" and, by implication, "unhealthy" forms of religion, depending on the psychological states they encouraged.[30]

That a person's (or a group's) use of religion could be unhealthy, to the point of triggering psychological and psychiatric conflict, was a major shift in emphasis from that of Peale's foundation and its evangelical religio-psychiatry. There treatment and conversion to Christianity had been thought to go hand in hand, and conversion was simply assumed to be beneficial. The academy instead drew heavily on Allport's research into religion and race prejudice, as well as the many psychological differences between "mature" and "immature" religiosity; the former was taken to be "well differentiated . . . dynamic in character . . . integral . . . and fundamentally heuristic" (problem solving), and the latter was of an unquestioning, "blindly institutional," and exclusionist kind.[31] Such distinctions led to considerable debate on whether "healthy" uses of religion could be separated from "unhealthy" ones, and if so, how. When, too, did religious belief result in moderation or extremism, including prejudice, and how might individuals— and the nation at large—best understand the difference?

"I always was . . .—and I am afraid I always shall be—suspicious of tying psychiatric problems in with religious ones." The comment reflects the fairly high degree of skepticism and frustration among scientists invited to the academy's first major symposium. "When emphasis is laid on the fact that religious life promotes mental health," continued Gregory Zilboorg, clinical professor of psychiatry at New York's College of Medicine, "I feel like warning myself to beware."[32]

The three-day affair had taken place in 1957 at a quiet retreat in Harriman State Park, north of New York City. Its banner topic, "Religion, Science, and Mental Health," was more than ambitious in scope; it felt historic. As its organizers noted, "Only a generation ago, a meeting of this kind would have been impossible."[33]

Yet among the core members present, and presumably among others, a complete and lasting convergence of religious and scientific perspectives turned out to be difficult. "It is true," the organizers noted, "that the scientists present were initially well-disposed toward religion, as the religionists were sympathetic to scientific investigation." But during the periods earmarked for discussion conflicts abounded, including how to reach consensus over quite different ways of defining the same thing. "Semantic difficulties produced annoyance at many points," the organizers conceded. "At times, it seemed they were a major block to communication."[34]

Perhaps for that reason, discussion became refreshingly candid. "It may . . . surprise us that religion is currently so often associated with mental well-being," commented Hans Hofmann, the clergyman directing Harvard's Project on Religion and Mental Health.[35] "I think we all want to identify religion and religious living with mental health," a second clergyman confirmed. Whether the evidence pointed in that direction was, he acknowledged, another matter entirely.[36]

To the question "Is there a relationship between people in total good health and religion?" the scientists attending contended that there was in fact "no very discernible relationship," and a clergyman claimed that he accepted the answer.[37] Later, Hofmann spoke of the "drugging effect of religious routine" and warned of the "false sense of security" that "erroneous religious attitudes" can foster.[38]

Noting that religions were far from alike in what they took to be mental health and ill health—a consideration that complicated and undermined Peale's religio-psychiatry—a psychiatrist at the symposium urged that future studies examine "what is common and what varies in the religious approaches" to these conditions.[39] A comparative focus on religion, involving empirical studies into a range of experiences, seemed promising. But a planned follow-up volume, "Religion and the Scientific Method," was quietly dropped from the list of future topics. The academy turned next to "Religion in the Developing Personality," a seemingly less contentious topic, and one closer to its founder's vision of health as religious harmony.[40]

Whether religious belief actually had an unambiguous relation to mental health was a question that surfaced repeatedly at the first symposium. If, as many participants observed, the *absence* of religious belief in an individual did not in itself imply mental weakness, ought the *presence* of belief be seen as conferring an intrinsic advantage? As a Protestant clergyman remarked, "I am assuming that it is possible to be mentally healthy as a Catholic, as a Protestant, as a Jew, as an atheist, as a Buddhist, or as anything else."[41]

Still, if mental health could be established quite independently of religion—a point the American Foundation of Religion and Psychiatry had strongly resisted, given its ongoing desire to fuse psychiatric treatment with religious conversion— why was "estrangement from God" still seen, at the academy, as an underlying *factor* in mental illness?[42] What justification remained for its continued religion-shaded definition of mental health?

Unlike at Peale's foundation, where discussion would at such points revert automatically to the assumed benefits of healing via faith, debate at the academy focused increasingly on a more open-ended but ultimately more rewarding matter: "What does religion really mean to people?"[43]

From that question flowed others: How do the devout interpret and live out the variety of traditions, urgings, and injunctions? What psychological profiles seem disposed to religious extremism? When might religious belief bolster resilience or accelerate recovery from loss? And how could the academy help distinguish between religious extremism and moderation?

Kenneth Appel, one of the academy's representatives, later spoke of the need for a cultural and individual "shift away from the rigidities of organized religion." He predicted a future, a decade hence, with an "increased tolerance of different faiths, different religions, agnosticism, lack of religion, and even anti-religion."[44] To him, secularism and atheism were not concerns. What was needed, he and other representatives of the academy stressed in 1965, was flexibility and receptivity among the nation's most devout and fundamentalist citizens for religious moderation to offset the risks and consequences of a faith based on fanaticism.

The emphasis on religious moderation and on maintaining—or rediscovering—a line between church and state was well timed. In 1962, despite ardent backing by conservative evangelicals, school prayer was struck down by the Supreme Court, which also ruled the following June against mandated Bible reading in public schools. Religious belief and its expression, Justice Tom Clark argued in the second decision, should be "free of any compulsion from the state."[45] In Idaho teachers had been daily required to read twelve to twenty verses of the Bible "without comment or interpretation," and a 1949 statute in Pennsylvania similarly required that teachers read "at least ten verses from the Holy Bible" to their classes each morning or risk being fired.[46]

Released from foundation responsibilities, Peale, meanwhile, took to defending President Nixon's self-conscious return to the public religiosity of the Eisenhower era (when Nixon had been vice president). Nixon's action was a sign of the direction that Peale and other evangelists would take as religious doctrines and tenets came under intense scrutiny. When charges sprang up that a president was once again seeking to fuse religion and politics in order to politicize religion, Peale was indignant. "The President would be appalled at the thought," he shot back as if personally informed. "The White House, after all, is Mr. Nixon's residence. And if there's anything improper about a man worshiping God in his own way in his own home, I'm at a loss to know what it is."[47]

With zealotry identified as one of the academy's concerns, attention turned to the sharp rise of scientism in American culture and the consequences of its often-uncompromising position on religion and religious belief. Scientism tended to view both as obstacles to mental health—at best as distractions and retrograde superstitions, at worst as forms of delusion involving an "escape from reality."[48]

At the academy symposium of 1957, participants repeatedly expressed frustration with a form of reductionism that psychiatry seemed increasingly to favor—that "man was nothing but" his biology or environment, instead of acknowledging a species that exhibited a history of metaphysical questioning and an almost universal quest for religious meaning. "What I call scientism," remarked Hofmann, "is one expectation that has deluded modern man into believing that merely through his scientific discoveries and technological advances he could eradicate all his difficulties and re-create the world and the people in it into a close approximation of his ideal of the way things should be."[49]

The Reverend Noël Mailloux, professor of psychology at the University of Montreal, amplified. One after another, he said, "we witnessed the sweeping invasions of Pavlovian reflexology, of behaviorism, of *Gestalt* theory, and, finally, of psychoanalysis, all displaying the same uncompromising and tightly impervious claims." Moreover, "we tended to forget that the total scope of a science is determined by its subject-matter, and not by any particular object falling within its sphere whose consideration may call for a different methodological approach."[50]

Even though scientists would disagree with Mailloux's contention that their inquiry is determined solely by known subject matter, the disputed and sometimes rancorous gray areas between religion and science led to a focus on what each could not do, at least in the eyes of the other, and what defied or eluded classification. "Science can only arrive at an objective relative description in its investigation of religious experiences," asserted Hofmann. "It cannot and should not want to attempt to reveal more than reflections on something that may be real but that is only at our disposition phenomenologically."[51]

Expanding on that key point to include Judaism as a culture and a philosophy, Rabbi Albert Goldman of Cincinnati summed up his beliefs with a challenge to the invited scientists:

I have here what I think is, at least for myself and for those who share this with me, an inner sense of security. I have a sense of knowing who I am and what part of myself I think is authentic to my nature, to my experience, to my background. It is not something I particularly care to break with, because it has become meaningful to me and to those around me.[52]

"It is not something I particularly care to break with." Beyond the strong influence of cultural ties and family history lay the powerful bonds and consolations of religion as the rabbi experienced them. The feeling they entailed was for him a hallmark of faith and persistence that would likely outlast scientific efforts at explaining it. It was, above all, a sentiment with which he had no desire to part.

The discussion took a decidedly testier turn when one of the participants alluded to the risk of "indoctrination" among the "religionists" (as they called themselves), including overuse of the word "indoctrination" itself. "I found myself increasingly uneasy last night at the frequent use of the word 'should,'" one medical educator remarked. "I kept feeling that a great deal of what was spoken of as education was not really that, but indoctrination."[53]

What was driving the imperatives seemed important to air. A clergyman tried to gloss the concern as referring to religious orthodoxy and blind adherence to creeds; but a Catholic priest, citing the customs and culture of his seminary, bristled at imputations that its teachings were in any way inflexible. "I think it must be realized that [in a seminary atmosphere] we have a different framework. . . . What I object to is that it seems to me you suggest that the necessary effort to do this is not education, but indoctrination."[54]

With an eye on the distinction between the two, Pope John XXIII opened the Second Vatican Council in 1962 with a mind to "reexamine old rigidities," as one foundation commentator put it, thereby altering "the general Roman Catholic outlook upon many things like psychiatry."[55] The idea was to end the type of hostility that Archbishop Fulton Sheen and other leading representatives of the Roman Catholic Church had voiced just a few years earlier when broadcasting warnings about psychiatry's and psychology's unhealthy preoccupation with the release of "lust," "carnality," and "concupiscence." "Not everyone in this world is cracked," the popular archbishop had exclaimed near the end of one 1957 lecture on "abnormality"; "we're reasonable beings, and we ought to know [that], and our leaders should tell us."[56] But religions of all kinds wanted to conserve, even to defend, a "different framework" in their theology and pastoral care, making it all but impossible to find lasting convergence between science and religion.

The organizers of the "Religion, Science, and Mental Health" symposium conceded that it was "only an initiating event." In truth, it was impressive that it took place at all.[57] The thaw in hostilities between the two groups was largely a result of "broadening outlooks on both sides."[58] The plight of the mentally ill had helped to keep the focus as much on practical difficulties as on puzzling abstractions. But the much-hoped-for consilience between the two groups had to wait for another day. What movement *had* taken place was more about the outward expansion of each side than about getting science and religion to align over something as complex and variously defined as mental health.

Although the academy had not solved the science-religion

conflict, it had lessened hostilities and accomplished much else—among other things, bringing to an end Peale's hold on religio-psychiatry. In addition to the training programs in mental health that the academy had developed at several religious seminaries, it had helped to upend a long-standing argument that religious belief *necessarily* implied psychological immaturity—an argument that an array of anthropologists, sociologists, and logical positivists had advanced with particular insistence since the 1920s and 1930s. (The claim itself was older still.)[59] What the academy instead developed was Allport's key distinction between two kinds of religiosity, fanaticism and moderation. The first of these supported only "self-serving" beliefs, whereas the second gave religion "an intrinsic value larger than self."[60]

This characterization of religiosity as both mature and immature upset some readers, since the terms implied a judgment that was highly susceptible to personal bias. Yet Allport, who chaired Harvard's Social Relations Department and was a past president of the American Psychological Association, did not mince words about the lengths to which a "literal-minded . . . compulsive religion" would go to uphold its own claims and deny those of others. Religious fanaticism of any kind is "fed by immature urgencies arising from unconscious forces," he argued in explaining the regional and sectarian differences that continued to surface nationally. The urgencies arose in ways that rendered religiosity itself "childish, authoritarian, and irrational."[61] Tolerance of different perspectives and religious customs was precisely what such extremism tried to rule out. "The religion of maturity makes the affirmation 'God is,' but only the religion of immaturity will insist, 'God is precisely what I say He is.'" With one eye on the nation's bitter struggle over civil rights and racial prejudice, including the de facto racial segregation of congregations across the South, Allport remarked of such extremists that their "sentiment stiffens and fights intolerantly all attempts to broaden it. In compulsive religion there is a defensive ruling-out of disturbing evidence."[62]

The distinction between compulsive and noncompulsive behavior would naturally hold for nonreligious settings, too. Fully aware that compulsivity had a life far beyond religious contexts, Allport was nonetheless insistent that his distinction included patterns of religious belief—that it was crucial for all religions to attend to their "shortcomings" and histories of extremism. About these he was blunt: "Religious wars, inquisitions, persecutions, and bigotry make a macabre spectacle. Perhaps he [the investigating religious moderate] will decide to abstain from the activities of institutional religion, as did Abraham Lincoln, who found its bickerings boresome and irrelevant to the mature mood of aspiration and wonder."[63]

Like the academy of which he was a part, Allport was keen to defend an individual's religious and spiritual striving. He noted that secularism left plenty of room for the "kind of religion [that] can steer one's existence without enslaving him to his limited conceptions and egocentric needs."[64] Through such distinctions, the highly regarded author and psychologist helped the academy—and the nation at large—redefine the very meaning of religious belief, from a sign of pro-American enthusiasm into a prized component of a person's psychological makeup.

No longer reduced to religious nationalism, magical thinking, or infantile projection, nor upheld as a necessary component of mental health, as the American Foundation of Religion and Psychiatry had argued, a person's private religion came to be seen by public intellectuals as a measure of reflection and maturity if it demonstrated an ability to tolerate religious differences and rein in extremism. Allport later modified his terms slightly to include discrepancies between merely rote or "institutionalized" beliefs and those that were more personalized or "intrinsic":

> Our hypothesis holds that, though religion of the extrinsic variety may hinder mental health, religion of the intrinsic variety may help. Each of us has known lives that remain serene in spite of inner turmoil, courageous in spite of the shattering shafts of fate. We have also known religious people who, in spite of neurotic fragments in their own lives, manage somehow to maintain control of their sanity—apparently because of a generic and embracing and guiding religious motive.[65]

What religion helped psychologically to maintain at such moments was, Allport postulated, more important than whether all such beliefs could be upheld as sound and plausible. The academy recognized that psychological well-being was the principal issue, even as it conceded that religion could have other effects, including the occasional instigation of a paralyzing sense of guilt or fear.

Because of personal temperament, but also because of cultural and religious shifts under way across much of the country (including toward spiritualism and away from religiosity), Allport focused on milder forms of religious conviction. He invoked persons who were "often heard to say, 'I don't know what I would do without religion'"—those for whom religious belief was "lockstitched into the whole fabric of being." To seek to remove or take away such a support would, he wrote, be "to cut much of the ground from under their existence."[66]

Given the range of other responses to loss of belief, including release from stricture and investigation into doctrine and dogma, Allport's warning may sound mildly overdramatized. Yet unlike commentators such as Princeton's Eric Goldman, who thought mockery and satire were better suited than religion to finding truth, and that support for religious moderation amounted to endorsing another person's bad faith, Allport pointed out that secular life was hardly free of illusions. "It is true that religion tends to define reality as congenial to the powers and aspirations of the individual," he conceded, "but so too does any working principle that sustains human endeavor. Those who find the religious principle of life illusory would do well not to scrutinize their own working principles too closely."[67]

Concerning the precise scientific help that religion could give to such moderates, Allport was frank: "We are still ignorant concerning the relation, if any, between mental soundness and the religious sentiment in a given life." He added later: "As of today, we have no firm evidence that religious people on the average are more mentally healthy than nonreligious people. What demographic differences there are indicate that income and education are far more important variables in mental health and illness than is personal religion—at least as personal religion is measured today (chiefly in terms of denominational affiliation)."[68]

A finer metric today records several health advantages among the religious: regular churchgoers on average live longer, are less likely to have heart attacks, and experience less anxiety and loneliness.[69] Allport was, however, detailing controversial news for the time—a connection between "institutionalized" religiosity and racial prejudice: "We have reported the finding that on the average, Church members seem to be *more* [racially] prejudiced than nonmembers" regarding support for the ongoing segregation of schools and churches, which Allport attributed to feeling in a "safe, powerful, [and economically] superior in-group." By contrast, those who had "interiorized" a religious outlook demonstrated markedly less prejudice and a stronger pull away from extremism.[70]

In Allport's studies of the social and psychological differences between "mature" and "immature" religiosity, the second finding—that higher levels of education and income in "interiorized" religion tended to *reduce* prejudice—lent credence to his and the academy's efforts at strengthening inquiry, tackling extremism, and fueling the search for a common understanding of vulnerable populations such as the mentally ill.[71] In light of that emphasis, the public and especially the political religiosity of the 1950s—of the kind Peale had done so much to fan and popularize—began to look increasingly exaggerated and contrived.

Coda
Faith as an Ongoing Force

The surge of piety that swept across the United States in the 1950s had not been primarily the result of a spontaneous explosion of religious feeling. Rather, it had stemmed from a concerted effort by Peale and other influential national figures to make it seem unhealthy and un-American to be unreligious.[1] Drawing religion deep into politics and the public sphere, as well as into science and definitions of mental health, Peale and others had presented religious beliefs as so integral to the country that the American way of life would seem unimaginable without them. The nation was encouraged to see itself as successful under God, its renewal and growing affluence a seeming consequence of religious commitment.

Eras of religious enthusiasm during American colonization date to at least the seventeenth century—religion, after all, is part of the founding story of the United States—and some eras then and since were significant for many and continue to define the nation's history.[2] Yet the ardent public religiosity of

the 1950s was different in kind and intensity, not least for involving the president and much of the Congress in "the dedication of our nation and our people to the Almighty."[3] In directing his message to Eisenhower and other close allies, Peale
had framed the message as faith in self, God, and country—
with faith in self seemingly an automatic expression of the
second and third faiths. With his sermons, broadcasts, and
best-selling books reaching Americans in the millions, Peale
had been well placed to encourage what he called "enthusiasm
for Christian world conquest."[4] His repeated appeals for "God
and gumption" had given belief in oneself religious significance. It had bound piety to mental health and made secularism appear not just deficient but at odds with normality. It
would take scholars and researchers almost two decades to
unstitch such claims and approach psychiatry and religion
with greater respect for their differences, but Peale's gospel of
religio-psychiatry found other pockets of support, including
among evangelists.

The rise in religious enthusiasm in the 1950s had done
much to alter relations between religion and science—psychiatry in particular, as we have seen. The American Foundation
of Religion and Psychiatry, a self-declared extension of Peale's
ministry, had taken to advising national leaders, corporations,
and doctors about the positive effects nationally of "com-
bin[ing] the discipline of psychiatry with the profound influence of God."[5] Pairing health with salvation, the Peale-Blanton
gospel had encouraged medicine to adopt a "proclamation of
faith" and patients to "accept religiously motivated ideas and
ideals." Throughout the religious boom of the 1950s, the foundation and its programs served as a key platform for the encounter between religion and science.[6]

In that much of the piety that had surged in the 1950s

declined almost as rapidly, many of the elements driving it
seem in hindsight geared to immediate influences and needs.
These include the heightened levels of fear and anxiety, dating
from the Great Depression but greatly intensified two decades
later by the threat of all-out nuclear war. Peale's message reso-
nated with a desire to strengthen national confidence and re-
assure postwar families anxious for stability while safeguard-
ing the nation against practical threats abroad. "By the early
1950s," the historian Ira Katznelson notes, "America's military
was *ten times* the size it had been in 1939, creating a new
political reality"—one that has aptly been called a "spiritual-
industrial complex."[7] The buildup was in response to communism, especially in the USSR under Stalin, and the Cold War
that had ensued.

As Peale's broader crusade for Americanism transitioned
from religious anticommunism to Christian nationalism, and
from religio-psychiatry to "practical" Christianity and self-
help, he had drawn in vast numbers of readers, listeners, and
worshippers. The postwar borderland between religion and
psychiatry had proven to be especially fertile ground for the
religious evangelicalism that would revolutionize political conservatism. Peale had urged Americans to believe that they
were capable of anything, but that mental and cultural health
were impossible without religious enthusiasm. The binding of
those elements had turned belief in self and country into religious imperatives; it had strengthened the idea that America
was a "redeemer" nation acting "under God."

To evangelical conservatives such as Peale, "communism
[could] only take root in a soil from which the religious ingre-
dient ha[d] been weakened or withdrawn," which was a key
reason why he had pressed for religiosity to take hold of and
unite the country.[8] We have seen how rapidly that emphasis

shifted to an assertion that religious faith was not just welcome but necessary for health and harmony. Equally palpable—and for a while compelling—was the cultural perception that it was somehow un-American to be unreligious.

The blending of affirmative psychology and religious belief that Peale had both encouraged and come to personify has had ongoing consequences for Americans. One is the softening of distinctions between positive psychology and positive theology; another is an expansion of the equation of health and religious salvation. For a sizable number of "megachurch" preachers and motivators the two elements are inseparable. Consider Joel Osteen, best-selling author and senior pastor at Houston's Lakewood Church. "You don't need God's help with small dreams," Osteen assures in *You Can, You Will: 8 Undeniable Qualities of a Winner* (2014), a title that might have been plucked from Peale's canon, though even more strident in its prosperity gospel. He urges: "Believe big. . . . Without a vision you won't see God's best. You won't be the winner He wants you to be."[9]

Osteen's church and media services, according to his publisher, are seen by more than ten million viewers each week in the United States alone. He doles out such bromides as "God will supersize your vision" and "When you are positive, hopeful, and expecting good things, you are in the jet stream of almighty God." Yet as with Peale's occasional slips into judgment and recrimination, the downside to such positivity is an easy, surprisingly rapid tumble into self-blame. "When you dwell on negative, defeated thoughts," the minister of today insists, "you poison your system. You are telling your command center, your mind—this incredible tool God has given you—to release defeat, failure, and mediocrity." To those merely dreaming more modestly, he adds, "They have programmed themselves for defeat."[10]

The idea, popularized by Peale, that religious faith is a personal and cultural *force* drives much of the upbeat message of Osteen and other contemporary preachers. Its roots, as we saw with Peale and Blanton's collaboration, extend to Freud's argument about the strength of transference, including to a saint or deity. The psychological principle rests firmly on a clear expectation of an improved outcome. In a medical setting, expecting remission or a cure can have profound and measurable physiological consequences. "In a broad sense," Ted Kaptchuk and Franklin Miller explain in the *New England Journal of Medicine,* "placebo effects are improvements in patients' symptoms that are attributable to their participation in the therapeutic encounter, with its rituals, symbols, and interactions."[11]

However, fueling such expectations on a mass scale within the terms of evangelical religio-psychiatry is not just risky but misleading and deceptive, as if half-counseling, half-preaching to the nation that religious faith was essential for the achievement of health and success. "When you are excellent," Osteen says, "your life gives praise to God." And on lesser days, when health or performance is less than optimal? The unwell, it is implied, have only themselves and weak faith to blame. They are too prone to release "defeat, failure, and mediocrity."[12]

One consequence of Freud's emphasis on transference is that the concept and the energy behind it are released from any necessary connection to religion. Charles McDonald, the inspiration for Blanton's earlier research, had insisted, "My expectations had become a certainty and the Blessed Virgin had healed me."[13] But without the requirement of a deity or a saint to validate transference, Freud brought the mechanism back down to earth; he encouraged assessment of its emotional power within relationships, among families, and even on nations—as a force behind conviction, fanaticism, and political movements such as Spiritual Mobilization.

"Belief in the *belief that something matters* is understandably strong and widespread." So notes the Tufts University cognitive scientist Daniel C. Dennett in his widely read 2006 polemic on religious belief, *Breaking the Spell*, regarding the assurance of hope that many derive from religion. "When you are faced with the often terrifying uncertainty of a dangerous world, the belief that *somebody* is *watching over you* may well be a decisively effective morale booster, capable of turning people who would otherwise be disabled by fear and indecision into stalwart agents."[14] Even those whose religious convictions waver or end may still retain "a firm belief that *belief in God* is something to preserve, so when they find the traditional concepts of God frankly incredible they don't give up. They seek a substitute. And the search . . . need not be all that conscious and deliberate."[15]

In *Breaking the Spell* Dennett hoped to demystify those responses to uncertainty and doubt, to redirect them to more secular aims: love of democracy, justice, and science, which happened to be Dennett's passions. With a keen focus on the specific consolations and assurances that religion offers the devout, he quoted the rational-choice theorists Rodney Stark and Roger Finke as indicating that the "draw" of religion is in this respect often rational and considered. For many believers, religion is "*the only plausible source of certain rewards for which there is a general and inexhaustible demand.*"[16] Dennett also grasped the importance of understanding how such beliefs look to those who hold them. "Why do people want to be stewards of their religions? It is obvious, isn't it? They believe that this is the way to lead a moral life, a good life, and they sincerely want to be good."[17]

"They sincerely want to be good." The generalization cannot hold for every zealot or fanatic. But especially when the resultant beliefs and actions are brought into the public sphere, that underlying desire has widespread social and psychological consequences that need assessing "whether or not any religious beliefs are *true*."[18] Dennett observed of one 2002 study on gauging the effects of religious beliefs empirically, including the effects on health and on religious movements: "There is no verdict yet on the hypothesis that intercessory prayer actually works ... but there is plenty of other evidence that active participation in religious organizations can improve the morale, and hence the health, of participants. Moreover, the defenders of religion can rightly point to less tangible but more substantial benefits to their adherents, such as having a meaning for their lives provided!"[19]

Research on the health issue has found further advantages in being devout: regular churchgoers on average experience less anxiety and loneliness than their nonreligious or nonobserving counterparts.[20] Add the scale of those benefits to Stark and Finke's point about the rational decisions that can underpin them, and the argument that such beliefs are a spell or delusion courts inaccuracy, even caricature. Dennett likened himself to the child in Hans Christian Andersen's fable who, by pointing to the naked emperor, succeeded in shattering his mystique and power. Nevertheless, the major religions persist, and millions still call themselves devout. "Shh. Don't break the spell," Dennett says with a wink to the reader elsewhere. Some belief systems he viewed as intrinsically "toxic": "these people need this crutch to keep their act together."[21]

In detailed polemics against religion and religious belief, the prolific neuroscientist Sam Harris has taken this argument further: "While religious people are not generally mad, their core beliefs absolutely are," he wrote in his 2004 best-seller, *The End of Faith*. He repeated his argument in an op-ed column directed at "God's Dupes."[22] Equally prominent among the "new atheists" is the biologist Richard Dawkins, who likens religious belief to psychosis in *The God Delusion* (2006), inveighs against "faith-heads," and declares faith "an evil."[23]

The reduction of religion to fanatical delusion doubtless serves polemic, but it hides a complex historical picture of argument, engagement, and compromise—even with religious moderates, as papers from the Academy of Religion and Mental Health show. Decades after the academy symposia came more scholarly advocates for "consilience" and "respectful noninterference" between science and religion, centrally E. O. Wilson (*Consilience*, 1998) and Stephen Jay Gould (*Rocks of Ages*, 1999). When their books appeared, an intense repolarization of antiscience evangelicals and scientific naturalists had made the gulf between these "non-overlapping magisteria" seem once more impossible to narrow or scale.[24]

We have seen how Blanton and Peale's advocacy for "religio-psychiatry" challenged the principle of "respectful noninterference," both in practice and through the very name "religio-psychiatry," as their foundation sought to make religious faith integral to American conceptions of mental health. Their archive serves as a cautionary tale about the consequences of integrating religion and science with regard to phenomena they interpret and describe quite differently.

By contrast, the Academy of Religion and Mental Health, with which the foundation eventually integrated, exemplifies

aspects of a contentious dialogue between science and religion
that historians and other scholars have not fully recognized,
including its effort to diminish their mutual antagonism.
Gordon Allport, who was closely tied to the academy, looked
to strengthen the ties with science among the population at
large. In 1954 he reported connections between religiosity
and prejudice while investigating how religious moderation
could weaken fanaticism.[25] Four years earlier, he had found
that moderates as a group were investigative, preoccupied by
evidence, and desirous of answers (even if they seemed to find
them within religion).[26]

The organizations at the center of this book initially took
quite different positions on the role of evangelicalism: Peale's
American Foundation of Religion and Psychiatry helped to
fuel the postwar "crusade" for Americanism by turning health
into a badge of religious conviction. By contrast, Allport and
the academy described religious extremism as a reason for the
continued antagonism between science and religion. They also
warned that positions so "uncompromising and tightly impervious" greatly reduced the possibility of dialogue and much-
needed cultural adjustment.[27]

In an excellent book on the polarities that have survived between antiscience evangelicals and scientific naturalists, the
philosopher David Ray Griffin describes the tendency of "par-
ties on both sides of a conflict to become fixated on an exag-
geration." Although "each position is giving witness to a truth,
in its exaggerated form this truth is a falsehood, because it
excludes the element of truth in the other position."[28] Dennett
and Harris take their polemic to intractable creationists and
literalists, rather than to the many theists who accepted—even
embraced—Darwinism while its founder was still alive.[29] Den-

nett preferred to marvel at the accuracy of quantum electro-dynamics rather than, say, some of the officially existing disorders that continue to dog American psychiatry.[30]

Part of the problem doubtless lies in the way religion and science are characterized and conceived. Scientific naturalism is often associated with atheism and determinism, given their shared precepts. Yet the philosophy does not require the underlying precepts of either belief system to be held as true. Griffin points out that accepting scientific naturalism needs only a rejection of supernaturalism; and Harris more recently called attention to the enormous conceptual space that is left for a category such as "spiritualism."[31] There is comparable movement on the religious side. For instance, large numbers of Christians consider the Bible apocryphally and metaphorically, without loss of faith, even if their acceptance of imprecision exasperates rationalists such as Dennett and Dawkins.[32]

Today America is pluralistic in belief and nonbelief, although many evangelical conservatives continue (as did Peale and his allies in the 1930s) to accuse the federal government of being too secular. The country is also religiously polarized, with mainstream *U.S. News and World Report* noting, during the 2004 presidential election (Kerry versus G. W. Bush), that to outsiders it must seem as if the nation's "churchgoers and secular voters live in parallel universes."[33] That schism has, if anything, widened in the years since. The sheer scale of difficulty that, for instance, the teaching of evolution and of climate science still represents in the United States makes the country an outlier among industrialized nations; its levels of religious observance are comparable to those of Turkey and Iran rather than of Britain or France.[34] (A third of Americans believe that scripture is the actual word of God, compared to 9 percent of Britons.)[35]

Nevertheless, an array of data signals that the United States is becoming less Christian and that evangelical conservatism is weakening as a political force.[36] "In every region of the country, in every Christian denomination," Adam Lee reported in the *Guardian* in October 2014, "membership is either stagnant or declining. Meanwhile, the number of religiously unaffiliated people—atheists, agnostics, those who are indifferent to religion, or those who follow no conventional faith—is growing. In some surprising places, these 'nones' (as in 'none of the above') now rank among the largest slices of the demographic pie."[37]

Extrapolating from the data, Lee refers to the so-called millennials, those born in the decades around the year 2000, with their signal diversity and tolerance, as "the least religious generation in American history—they are even getting less religious as they get older, which is unprecedented—and the majority of them identify Christianity as synonymous with harsh political conservatism."[38] The nonpartisan Pew Research Center underlined that trend and association in May 2015, reporting that the number of Americans who identified as Christian had fallen almost eight percentage points between 2007 and 2014. During that time, five million fewer Americans identified as Christian even as the number of Americans who identified themselves as having no religion grew from 16 percent to 23 percent. This last move made nonobserving Americans the second largest group in the country (after evangelicals) as defined by religion or its absence.[39]

"Godless millennials"—Lee's phrase—may be "spiritual," the data indicate, but they are not conventionally "religious" in the sense of being connected with traditional religious organizations. Significantly, the same powerful currents in religious belief and nonbelief are thus likely to impact millennials' conceptions of health and to release them from any obvious or necessary connection to religious enthusiasm.

Evangelical Christians nonetheless remain the nation's largest religious group. As Robert Putnam and David Campbell note in *American Grace: How Religion Divides and Unites Us* (2010), many of them align themselves with conservatism ("theological, social, moral, and political") while adopting stringent antiscience positions across a variety of topics.[40] Given the consequences of such diametrically held positions, the continued standoff across the country is risky, with all sides maintaining claims so "uncompromising and tightly impervious" that no real dialogue or adjustment is possible. As with the new atheists' pairing of religious belief with delusion and of moderation with complicity, such characterizations paralyze action and policy. They harden polarities and reduce much of the culture to a state of low-simmering hostility.

The rejection of antiscience evangelicalism by religious moderates and by godless millennials signals where the lines of engagement are being productively redrawn. To persist in claiming, as do evangelicals in the age of ratiometric dating, that the planet is less than ten thousand years old is one sign of the difficulty. Likening the religious to "faith-heads" and belief to psychosis is equally likely to leave extremism intact. A more complex engagement is necessary to determine what religion really means to people. The alternative? The nation remains divided, with no productive dialogue between church-going and secular citizens. The gung-ho pro-democracy Peale would not approve.

Notes

Introduction

1. "'Christ or Marx' Issue of Hour, Says Dr. Peale. U.S. Must Choose between Church and the Reds, He Declares in Sermon," *New York Herald Tribune,* January 20, 1936.

2. See also "Christianity Seen in Race with Chaos. Final Destiny of Civilization in Our World Is the Prize, Dr. N. V. Peale Declares," *New York Times,* April 11, 1938.

3. "Clergyman Scores County Politicians for Their Betrayal of Religion," *Syracuse Journal,* March 23, 1931.

4. Norman Vincent Peale to Edward F. Hutton, July 21, 1947, Norman Vincent Peale Papers, Special Collections Research Center, Syracuse University Libraries (hereafter "NVP papers"). Comparable statements to other close associates are detailed in Chapter 3.

5. J. Ronald Oakley, *God's Country: America in the Fifties* (New York: Barricade, 1990), 323.

6. Ira Katznelson, *Fear Itself: The New Deal and the Origins of Our Time* (New York: Liveright, 2013), 13. Roosevelt is quoted on 274.

7. Ibid., 3.

8. Peale to Hutton, July 21, 1947; Peale, as quoted in "Enthusiasm Need for Conquest of Christian World," *Syracuse Post-Standard,* July 2, 1928.

9. "Labor Is Warned of 'Foreign' Taint. Peale Fears 'Red' Aspect of Agitation Is a Token of Un-American Trends. Deplores Bitter Spirit," *New York*

Times, January 18, 1937; "Peale Sees Nation in New Revolution," *New York Times,* January 8, 1934.

10. "Peale Sees Nation in New Revolution."

11. Kevin M. Kruse, *One Nation under God: How Corporate America Invented Christian America* (New York: Basic Books, 2015), 6.

12. H. W. Prentis, Jr., "Our American Heritage: Revive Patriotism and Religious Faith," speech before the general session of the U.S. Chamber of Commerce, Washington, D.C., May 4, 1939, reprinted in *Vital Speeches of the Day,* June 15, 1939, 519 and 521.

13. Dr. James W. Fifield, Jr., "America's Future" (May 1938), as quoted in Kruse, *One Nation under God,* 12.

14. Ad for Spiritual Mobilization, *Los Angeles Times,* December 23, 1939; Dr. James W. Fifield, Jr., Tenth Fall Bulletin, Spiritual Mobilization, [1944], as quoted in Kruse, *One Nation Under God,* 11–12.

15. Kevin M. Kruse, "For God So Loved the One Percent . . ." *New York Times,* January 18, 2012. See also William C. Martin, *With God on Our Side: The Rise of the Religious Right in America* (New York: Broadway Books, 1996); Martin E. Marty, *Modern American Religion,* vol. 3: *Under God, Indivisible: 1941–1960* (Chicago: University of Chicago Press, 1996); and Leo Ribuffo, *The Old Christian Right: The Protestant Far Right from the Great Depression to the Cold War* (Philadelphia: Temple University Press, 1983), especially chapter 1.

16. "Public Officials Require Watching, Pastor Warns . . . Criticizes Roosevelt's 'Indifference to Religion': Dr. Peale Calls It Cause of Vital New Deal Errors," *New York Herald Tribune,* August 19, 1935; "Love of Deity Loyalty Test," *Syracuse Post-Standard,* February 18, 1929.

17. J. Edgar Hoover, as quoted in Richard G. Powers, *Not without Honor: The History of American Anticommunism* (New Haven: Yale University Press, 1998), 217, 216; "'Christ or Marx' Issue of Hour, Says Dr. Peale."

18. Louis C. Rabaut (D-Michigan), U.S. Congress, House, 83rd Cong., 2nd Sess., *Congressional Record,* February 12, 1954, 1700.

19. "The President's Prayer," *Los Angeles Times,* January 21, 1953.

20. Kruse, *One Nation under God,* 6, 14, 17–18.

21. Ad by the Committee to Proclaim Liberty (1951), sponsored by the San Diego Gas and Electric Company, as quoted in Kruse, *One Nation under God,* 30.

22. Dr. James W. Fifield, Jr., *The Cross vs. the Sickle* (Los Angeles: First Congregational Church, July 1947), NVP papers.

23. *The Sickle or the Cross,* dir. Frank R. Strayer (74 mins., black and white), released July 1, 1949; later rereleased as *Seeds of Destruction.*

24. Billy Graham, as quoted in Peter Lewis, *The Fifties* (New York: Lippincott, 1978), 73–74. For an extended focus on the period's anticommunism, see David Caute, *The Great Fear: The Anti-Communist Purge under Truman and Eisenhower* (New York: Simon and Schuster, 1978); Ellen Schrecker, *Many Are the Crimes: McCarthyism in America* (Boston: Little, Brown, 1998); and Jessica Wang, *American Science in an Age of Anxiety: Scientists, Anticommunism, and the Cold War* (Chapel Hill: University of North Carolina Press, 1999).

25. "Ike Says Faith Keeps Him Going: He'd Crack without It," *New York World-Telegram and Sun*, November 8, 1957; "Eisenhower Calls Faith His Shield: Saves Him from Mental Hospital," undated newspaper clipping in NVP papers.

26. President-elect Eisenhower, speaking extemporaneously on December 22, 1952, as quoted in Patrick Henry, "'And I Don't Care What It Is': The Tradition-History of a Civil Religion Proof-Text," *Journal of the American Academy of Religion* 49.1 (March 1981), 41.

27. Eisenhower, as quoted in William Lee Miller, *Piety along the Potomac: Notes on Politics and Morals in the '50s* (Boston: Houghton Mifflin, 1964), 21.

28. Eisenhower, as quoted in "God in the White House," material related to the PBS documentary *God in America*, October 2010.

29. Ibid.

30. Miller, *Piety along the Potomac*.

31. Jonathan P. Herzog, *The Spiritual-Industrial Complex: America's Religious Battle against Communism in the Early Cold War* (New York: Oxford University Press, 2011), 3, quoting *Chaplains' Character Guidance Manual for Training Divisions and Training Centers* (Carlisle Barracks, Pa.: The Chaplain School of the United States Army, n.d.); Jean Franco, *The Decline and Fall of the Lettered City: Latin America in the Cold War* (Cambridge, Mass.: Harvard University Press, 2002), 22. See also Andrew Preston, *Sword of the Spirit, Shield of Faith: Religion in American War and Diplomacy* (New York: Anchor Books, 2012), 440–64; and T. Jeremy Gunn, *Spiritual Weapons: The Cold War and the Forging of an American National Religion* (Westport, Conn.: Praeger, 2008).

32. Hoover, as quoted in Douglas T. Miller and Marion Nowak, *The Fifties: The Way We Really Were* (New York: Doubleday, 1977), 91.

33. On October 19, 1954, for instance, Peale wrote to thank Hoover for "the tremendously important work which you are doing for God and for our country. . . . You are held in esteem, almost veneration, by the people and I feel that you [*sic*] great message of Americanism plus sound Christian faith

is something everyone needs, especially at the present time." On December 20, 1956, Peale said further: "God has called you to your position, just as certainly as any minister has been called to the pulpit, and you have been a faithful servant" (both in NVP papers). Hoover was flattered, and quick to agree with such claims.

34. Kruse, *One Nation under God,* 68.

35. Oakley, *God's Country,* 325.

36. Even in quieter though still wildly popular films such as *A Man Called Peter* (dir. Henry Koster, 1955), itself based on a best-selling book, Peter Marshall, as newly appointed chaplain to Congress, is filmed urging from the Senate floor: "Help us make this God's own country by living like God's own people." See also Peter Marshall, "Sanctify Our Love of Country," in Catherine Marshall, *A Man Called Peter: The Story of Peter Marshall* (New York: McGraw-Hill, 1951), 293.

37. Cecil B. DeMille, as quoted in "New Lore Enriches 'Ten Commandments,'" *Los Angeles Times,* February 12, 1956.

38. According to Kruse, "nearly four thousand monuments" were established nationally (*One Nation under God,* 148).

39. Norman Vincent Peale, "Let the Church Speak Up for Capitalism," *Reader's Digest,* September 1950, 128.

40. Miller, *Piety along the Potomac,* 134; Ron Alexander, "Chronicle," *New York Times,* May 31, 1994.

41. The sales figures are according to the book's paperback publisher, Fireside, an imprint of Simon and Schuster. Such numbers contradict greatly exaggerated claims that the book has been translated into forty-two languages and has, according to some sources, sold as many as twenty-one million copies. See, for example, the obituary for Peale's wife, Ruth Stafford Peale: "Pastor's Wife Co-Founded *Guideposts*," *Los Angeles Times,* February 8, 2008.

42. "Dr. Peale Sees Faith as Source of Power," *New York American,* February 3, 1936.

43. American Foundation of Religion and Psychiatry Development Fund, "Toward Mental Health for All," undated fund-raising brochure [1955], Institutes of Religion and Health Records, Special Collections Research Center, Syracuse University Libraries (hereafter "IRH papers").

44. "Religio-Psychiatric Clinic of the Marble Collegiate Church," undated brochure; and American Foundation of Religion and Psychiatry, "A Religious Outlook on Life," in *Service of Worship for Healing,* Confidential minutes to Administrative Meetings, November 27, 1960, 4, both in IRH papers.

45. David E. Roberts, "Health from the Standpoint of the Christian Faith," in Paul B. Maves, ed., *The Church and Mental Health* (New York: Scribner's, 1953), 23. The Academy of Religion and Mental Health also drew on this definition.

46. Sigmund Freud, as quoted on the jacket of Sigmund Freud, *Psychoanalysis and Faith: Dialogues with the Reverend Oskar Pfister*, ed. Heinrich Meng and Ernst L. Freud, trans. Eric Mosbacher (New York: Basic Books, 1963).

47. Samuel Z. Klausner, "The Religio-Psychiatric Movement: Changing Ideology of the Movement (Lecture II)," *Review of Religious Research* 6.1 (1964), 22.

48. "Peale, President Address FBI Class," *Washington Post and Times Herald*, November 9, 1957.

49. "Research—1. In Religion and Psychiatry," document attached to a letter from John M. Cotton (Chair, Research Committee, American Foundation of Religion and Psychiatry) to Dr. Bernard Barber (Professor of Sociology, Barnard College), February 13, 1959, IRH papers. For amplification of the history of such thinking, see Samuel Z. Klausner, "The Religio-Psychiatric Movement (Lecture I)," *Review of Religious Research* 5.2 (1964), 63–74; and E. Brooks Holifield, *A History of Pastoral Care in America: From Salvation to Self-Realization* (Nashville, Tenn.: Abingdon Press, 1983), chapter 7.

50. "Research—1. In Religion and Psychiatry."

51. Norman Vincent Peale with Elmer Hess, M.D., president of the American Medical Association, *Medicine's Proclamation of Faith* (Atlantic City, N.J., June 7, 1955), IRH papers.

52. Norman Vincent Peale, as quoted in the obituary "Norman Vincent Peale Dies in His Sleep at 95," Associated Press, December 26, 1993; Peale, *The Power of Positive Thinking* (1952; New York: Fireside, 2003), xiii.

53. Jacket of Norman Vincent Peale and Smiley Blanton, *Faith Is the Answer: A Pastor and a Psychiatrist Discuss Your Problems* (1940; Carmel, N.Y.: Guideposts, 1955).

54. Oral Roberts and G. H. Montgomery, eds., *God's Formula for Success and Prosperity* (Tulsa, Okla.: Oral Roberts, 1955); Eric Goldman, "Good-by to the Fifties—and Good Riddance," *Harper's Magazine* 220 (January 1960), 28.

55. Gregory Zilboorg, as quoted in Academy of Religion and Mental Health, *Religion, Science, and Mental Health: Proceedings of the First Academy Symposium on Inter-discipline Responsibility for Mental Health—A Religious and Scientific Concern, 1957* (New York: New York University Press, 1959), 31.

56. Confidential minutes to Administrative Meeting, November 27, 1960, IRH papers.

57. Robert D. Putnam and David E. Campbell, *American Grace: How Religion Divides and Unites Us* (New York: Simon and Schuster, 2010), 100.

58. The organization briefly formed from the merger was the Institutes of Religion and Health (1972–75), whose practical arm remains the Blanton-Peale Institute and Counseling Center in New York City.

59. See, for instance, "U.S. Rep. Paul Broun: Evolution a Lie 'from the Pit of Hell,'" *Los Angeles Times,* October 7, 2012. At the time, Broun (R-Georgia) sat on the Science, Space, and Technology Committee of the House.

60. Richard Dawkins, "How Dare You Call Me a Fundamentalist: The Right to Criticise 'Faith-Heads,'" *Times* (London), May 12, 2007; Dawkins, *The God Delusion* (Boston: Houghton Mifflin, 2006), 308.

61. Sam Harris, *The End of Faith: Religion, Terror, and the Future of Reason* (New York: Norton, 2004), 73, emphasis in original; Harris, "God's Dupes," *Los Angeles Times,* March 15, 2007. See also, more recently, Harris, *Waking Up: A Guide to Spirituality without Religion* (New York: Simon and Schuster, 2014). A best-seller, *The End of Faith* was instrumental in setting out Harris's position that faith was by definition irrational and people with faith were in a state bordering on mental illness.

62. Daniel C. Dennett, *Breaking the Spell: Religion as a Natural Phenomenon* (New York: Penguin, 2006), 21, 207, 334.

1

Religio-Psychiatry Arrives in New York

1. Norman Vincent Peale and Smiley Blanton, *The Art of Real Happiness* (New York: Prentice Hall, 1950), 5.

2. "Research—1. In Religion and Psychiatry," document attached to a letter from John M. Cotton (chair, research committee, American Foundation of Religion and Psychiatry) to Dr. Bernard Barber (professor of sociology, Barnard College), February 13, 1959, Institutes of Religion and Health Records, Special Collections Research Center, Syracuse University Libraries (hereafter "IRH papers"). At the time, Barber worked at the Bureau of Applied Social Research, Columbia University, an organization the foundation solicited repeatedly for assistance in validating its research program.

3. Norman Vincent Peale, "Science of a Satisfying Life," *NBC Network,* December 9, 1951, text of a radio address in Norman Vincent Peale Papers,

Special Collections Research Center, Syracuse University Libraries (hereafter "NVP papers").

4. "Healing and Research Program," undated document, IRH papers.

5. American Foundation of Religion and Psychiatry Board Meeting minutes, April 5, 1961, IRH papers.

6. A. Roy Eckardt, *The Surge of Piety in America: An Appraisal* (New York: Association Press, 1958).

7. "Peale Optimistic about Future: Hails 'Spiritual Awakening,'" *Kalamazoo Gazette*, undated clipping in NVP papers.

8. Arthur Schlesinger, Jr., *The Age of Roosevelt*, vol. 3: *The Politics of Upheaval: 1935–1936* (Boston: Houghton Mifflin, 1960), 656.

9. Ward James, a teacher, as quoted in Studs Terkel, *Hard Times: An Oral History of the Great Depression* (New York: Pantheon, 1970), 423.

10. See, for instance, Smiley Blanton to Norman Vincent Peale, March 1 and April 4, 1950, IRH papers, quoted in Chapter 5.

11. Peale and Blanton, *The Art of Real Happiness*, 6.

12. Samuel Z. Klausner, *Psychiatry and Religion: A Sociological Study of the New Alliance of Ministers and Psychiatrists* (Glencoe, Ill.: Free Press, 1964), 198, 202.

13. Jennifer Priddy, "The History of Blanton-Peale: 1935–1993," unpublished essay (December 8, 1993), 1, Blanton-Peale Institute and Counseling Center, New York City; Norman Vincent Peale, *This Incredible Century* (Wheaton, Ill.: Living Books, 1991), 138–39.

14. "Conclusion," in Rev. Arthur M. Tingue, Report of Executive Director to the Board of Directors, May 4, 1966, IRH papers.

15. Peale, characterizing Blanton's words and sentiment, in *This Incredible Century*, 139.

16. "Religious Healing" and "Research—1. In Religion and Psychiatry," IRH papers; Blanton, as quoted in Peale, *This Incredible Century*, 140.

17. Rev. Arthur M. Tingue, Report of Executive Director to the Board of Directors, American Foundation of Religion and Psychiatry, November 5, 1964, IRH papers.

18. *Trends and Issues in Psychiatric Residency Programs: Report 31* (Topeka, Kans.: Group for the Advancement of Psychiatry, 1955), 1. See also, as an equally influential follow-up, John Feighner et al., "Diagnostic Criteria for Use in Psychiatric Research," *Archives of General Psychiatry* 26.1 (1972), 57–63.

19. Karl Menninger, M.D., "Psychiatry," in Harold E. Stearns, ed., *America Now: An Inquiry into Civilization in the United States* (New York: Scribner's,

1938), 425–55; Menninger, foreword to Robert G. Gassert and Bernard H. Hall, *Psychiatry and Religious Faith* (New York: Viking Press, 1964), xiv.

20. "Dr. Fred C. Schwarz, Noted Surgeon, Psychiatrist," as quoted in Kevin M. Kruse, *One Nation under God: How Corporate America Invented Christian America* (New York: Basic Books, 2015), 148–49. See also "Why a Christian Cannot Be a Communist," referenced and discussed in Jonathan P. Herzog, *The Spiritual-Industrial Complex: America's Religious Battle against Communism in the Early Cold War* (New York: Oxford University Press, 2011), ix.

21. Joshua L. Liebman, *Peace of Mind* (New York: Simon and Schuster, 1946); Fulton J. Sheen, *Peace of Soul* (New York: Whittlesey House, 1949); Billy Graham, *Peace with God* (New York: Doubleday, 1953). Liebman, in particular, joined Peale in tying religious faith to positive psychology, although the roots of that pairing extend far into nineteenth-century New Thought. See, for instance, Donald Meyer, *The Positive Thinkers: A Study of the American Quest for Health, Wealth and Personal Power from Mary Baker Eddy to Norman Vincent Peale* (Garden City, N.Y.: Doubleday, 1965); and Andrew R. Heinze, "*Peace of Mind* (1946): Judaism and the Therapeutic Polemics of Postwar America," *Religion and American Culture* 12.1 (2002), 31–58.

22. Like Peale and Graham, Sheen drew extensively on anticommunism for his conservative-religious vision. See, for instance, Fulton J. Sheen, *Communism Answers Questions of a Communist* (New York: Paulist Press, 1936); and, for Catholicism's broader role in advancing religious anticommunism, Herzog, *The Spiritual-Industrial Complex*, 55–66.

23. Carol V. R. George, *God's Salesman: Norman Vincent Peale and the Power of Positive Thinking* (New York: Oxford University Press, 1993), 123.

24. For instance, the psychologist Fredric Wertham, "Short-Cut to Joy," *Saturday Review*, April 22, 1950, 21; and the psychiatrist Robert C. Murphy, Jr., "Think Right! Reverend Peale's Panacea," *The Nation*, May 7, 1955, 398.

25. "Public Officials Require Watching, Pastor Warns . . . Criticizes Roosevelt's 'Indifference to Religion': Dr. Peale Calls It Cause of Vital New Deal Errors," *New York Herald Tribune*, August 19, 1935, 9.

26. Vivian Kellens to Norman Vincent Peale, December 7, 1950, NVP papers.

27. Margaret W. Harrison to Norman Vincent Peale, January 5, 1951, NVP papers.

28. Ibid.

29. Norman Vincent Peale to V[ivian] Kellens, December 13, 1950, NVP papers.

30. Margaret Gray Blanton, "Biographical Notes and Comments," in Smiley Blanton, *Diary of My Analysis with Sigmund Freud* (New York: Hawthorn, 1971), 122; S. Blanton, as quoted in Peale, *This Incredible Century*, 140.

31. S. Blanton, *Diary*, 86; and S. Blanton as quoted in Peale, *This Incredible Century*, 140.

32. Staff Credo, attached to minutes of meeting of Board of Directors, June 12, 1957, IRH papers.

33. "Lord dismiss us with Thy blessing" (Hymn no. 65), in Program of Dedication of Headquarters of the Religio-Psychiatric Clinic and the Pastoral Training Program at the Marble Collegiate Church, October 19, 1955, IRH papers.

34. Fred Tate, statement as director of clinical services, in "The Role of Religion," June 12, 1957, IRH papers.

35. Tingue, Report of Executive Director to the Board of Directors, November 5, 1964.

36. Stephen G. Prichard, director of development, "The Relationship of Religion, Psychiatry, and Christian Ethics," in "The Role of Religion," 2.

37. Ibid. For more on these assumptions, see Donald Capps, "Norman Vincent Peale, Smiley Blanton and the Hidden Energies of the Mind," *Journal of Religion and Health* 48.4 (2009), 507–27; and Stephanie Muravchik, *American Protestantism in the Age of Psychology* (New York: Cambridge University Press, 2011), especially chapters 1 and 3.

38. Roland R. Reed, assistant director of training, "What Is the Religious Dimension of Pastoral Counseling?," in "The Role of Religion," 1.

39. Tate, statement as director of clinical services, in "The Role of Religion," 1.

40. Prichard, "The Relationship of Religion, Psychiatry, and Christian Ethics," in "The Role of Religion," 2.

41. American Foundation of Religion and Psychiatry, "A Religious Outlook on Life," in *Service of Worship for Healing*, IRH papers.

42. Peale and Blanton, *The Art of Real Happiness*, 7.

43. Peale's secretary to Peale, regarding an attached letter from Mrs. Picker to Peale, June 9, 1946, NVP papers.

44. Peale and Blanton, *The Art of Real Happiness*, 8, 9.

45. Norman Vincent Peale to Smiley Blanton, April 30, 1952, IRH papers.

46. Ibid., with "Case No. 1" attached.

47. Peale and Blanton, *The Art of Real Happiness*, 9.

48. See, for instance, Murphy, "Think Right!" 398–400; and William Lee

Miller, "Some Negative Thinking about Norman Vincent Peale," ·in *Piety along the Potomac: Notes on Politics and Morals in the '50s* (Boston: Houghton Mifflin, 1964), 136–40 (first published in *The Reporter,* January 13, 1955).

49. Klausner, *Psychiatry and Religion,* 202.

50. Patient information form attached to report of the Statistic Committee, in minutes of the Administrative Committee Meeting, July 30, 1963, IRH papers.

51. Confidential supplement to the minutes of the Administrative Committee Meeting, February 4, 1962, IRH papers.

52. The Religio-Psychiatric Clinic, American Foundation of Religion and Psychiatry facts, updated November 12, 1957, 2, IRH papers.

53. "Client Problems Presented to Clinic of American Foundation of Religion and Psychiatry, Inc." (1955), IRH papers.

54. Klausner, *Psychiatry and Religion,* 203. Elizabeth "Lyons" was in fact noted in all foundation literature as Elizabeth R. Lyon, without a final "s."

55. Smiley Blanton, in "Unfinished Business—The Relation of Religion and Psychiatry," minutes of the Executive Committee Meeting, September 30, 1963, IRH papers.

56. Peale and Blanton, *The Art of Real Happiness,* 3; Smiley Blanton to Norman Vincent Peale, March 18, 1960, IRH papers.

57. "Of the Millions Who Live—Only a Few Are Remembered!" undated promotional brochure for the American Foundation of Religion and Psychiatry (1960s), IRH papers.

58. Smiley Blanton to Norman Vincent Peale, January 9, 1962, IRH papers. The letter was designed to counter Peale's concern that he had done "irreparable" harm to his reputation by asserting that a Catholic such as John F. Kennedy should never be president, given his loyalty to Rome. Blanton concluded: "I can only pray, Norman, that you can accept your anxiety and feelings of inadequacy and realize they are due to some childish conflict and have very little to do with reality, at the present time."

59. See Millais Culpin, "The Conception of Nervous Disorder," *British Journal of Medical Psychology* 35 (1962), 73–80; and Fay Bound, "Anxiety: Keywords in the History of Medicine," *The Lancet* 363 (April 24, 2004), 1407.

60. The phrase is taken from Wertham, "Short-Cut to Joy," 21; but for the "birth of a psychiatric style of reasoning," see also Arnold I. Davidson, *The Emergence of Sexuality: Historical Epistemology and the Formation of Concepts* (Cambridge, Mass.: Harvard University Press, 2002), especially 36–37, 137.

61. Peale and Blanton, *The Art of Real Happiness,* 9.

2
On the Couch with Freud

1. Norman Vincent Peale and Smiley Blanton, *The Art of Real Happiness* (New York: Prentice Hall, 1950), 9.

2. Sigmund Freud, as quoted in Smiley Blanton, *Diary of My Analysis with Sigmund Freud* (New York: Hawthorn, 1971), 84.

3. Margaret Gray Blanton, editorial note, in S. Blanton, *Diary,* 99.

4. S. Blanton, *Diary,* 84.

5. Ibid., 98.

6. M. Blanton, preface to S. Blanton, *Diary,* 9.

7. S. Blanton, *Diary,* 80–81.

8. Ibid., 68.

9. Ibid., 54.

10. Ibid., 67, 71, 73.

11. Ibid., 84.

12. S. Blanton, as quoted in Norman Vincent Peale, *This Incredible Century* (Wheaton, Ill.: Living Books, 1991), 140.

13. S. Blanton, *Diary,* 114.

14. Ibid., 86.

15. Ibid., 15, 113.

16. Ibid., 113, 86.

17. Harriet Hall, "The Placebo Effect," *Skeptic,* May 20, 2009, http://www.skeptic.com/. See also Ted J. Kaptchuk and Franklin G. Miller, "Placebo Effects in Medicine," *New England Journal of Medicine* 373.8–9 (July 2015), doi:10.1056/NEJMp1504023; Susan Huculak, "The Placebo Effect in Psychiatry: Problem or Solution?" *Journal of Medical Ethics* 40.6 (2014), 376–80, doi:10.1136/medethics-2013-101410; and Azgad Gold and Pesach Lichtenberg, "The Moral Case for the Clinical Placebo," *Journal of Medical Ethics* 40.4 (2014), 219–24, doi:10.1136/medethics-2012-101314.

18. S. Blanton, *Diary,* 97.

19. Ibid., 104.

20. Ibid.

21. Ibid., 112.

22. In his *Diary,* Blanton notes that Freud said: "Faith represents a childish relation to the parent. To be sure, when it is to others, it may be, as you say, a transference of this parental faith to them" (97).

23. Smiley Blanton, note to Dr. Iago Galdston, November 2, 1956, Institutes of Religion and Health Records, Special Collections Research Center, Syracuse University Libraries (hereafter "IRH papers").

24. Peale and Blanton, *The Art of Real Happiness*, 12; Norman Vincent Peale, *The Power of Positive Thinking* (1952; New York: Fireside, 2003), 174.

25. Jonathan P. Herzog, *The Spiritual-Industrial Complex: America's Religious Battle against Communism in the Early Cold War* (New York: Oxford University Press, 2011), 3–7.

26. Smiley Blanton, "Analytical Study of a Cure at Lourdes," *Psychoanalytic Quarterly* 9 (1940), 362, 361.

27. Ibid., 362, 358.

28. Ibid., 360–61.

29. Ibid., 351.

30. Ibid., 351–52.

31. Ibid., 352.

32. Ibid., 348.

33. Ibid., 355, quoting Dr. Young (September 1937).

34. Ibid., 358.

35. Ibid., 353, quoting Charles McDonald.

36. S. Blanton, *Diary*, 105, 112.

37. Sigmund Freud, *Civilization and Its Discontents* (1929, rev. 1930; New York: Norton, 1961), 72–73.

38. Smiley Blanton, "Freud and Theology," *The Pastoral Counselor* 1.2 (1963), 3.

39. Sigmund Freud, *The Future of an Illusion* (1927; New York: Norton, 1961), 43, 49, 44.

40. Sigmund Freud to Rev. Oskar Pfister, February 9, 1909, in Sigmund Freud, *Psychoanalysis and Faith: Dialogues with the Reverend Oskar Pfister*, ed. Heinrich Meng and Ernst L. Freud, trans. Eric Mosbacher (New York: Basic Books, 1963), 17.

41. Freud, *The Future of an Illusion*, 37.

42. Freud to Pfister, May 10, 1909, and November 25, 1928, in Freud, *Psychoanalysis and Faith*, 24 and 126, emphasis in original.

43. Freud to Pfister, February 2, 1909, in Freud, *Psychoanalysis and Faith*, 16–17. See also 118: "however warm-heartedly the analyst may behave, he cannot set himself up in the analysand's mind as a substitute for God and providence."

44. Freud to Pfister, February 7, 1930, in Freud, *Psychoanalysis and Faith*, 133.

45. Freud, *The Future of an Illusion*, 49, 19.

46. Freud, *The Future of an Illusion*, 49.

47. Carol V. R. George, *God's Salesman: Norman Vincent Peale and the Power of Positive Thinking* (New York: Oxford University Press, 1993), 21, 22.

48. Freud, as quoted in S. Blanton, *Diary,* 76.

49. Smiley Blanton, "Dr. Freud for the Pulpit," *New York Herald Tribune,* October 23, 1949; Rev. R. S. Lee, *Freud and Christianity* (New York: A. A. Wyn, 1949), 79.

50. S. Blanton, "Dr. Freud for the Pulpit."

51. Norman Vincent Peale and Smiley Blanton, *Faith Is the Answer: A Pastor and a Psychiatrist Discuss Your Problems* (1940; Carmel, N.Y: Guideposts, 1955), v.

52. Smiley Blanton, "The Power of Faith," in Peale and Blanton, *Faith Is the Answer,* 3. In the first (1940) edition, unlike in the two later ones, Blanton's name appears before Peale's.

53. Norman Vincent Peale, "Grief and Sorrow," in Peale and Blanton, *Faith Is the Answer,* 157.

54. Peale, "Self-Criticism, Failure, and Success," in Peale and Blanton, *Faith Is the Answer,* 132.

55. Peale and Blanton, "Learning to Pray Effectively," in Peale and Blanton, *Faith Is the Answer,* 269.

56. Ibid., 266, 268.

57. Norman Vincent Peale to an anonymous reader in *Look,* October 1956.

58. Mrs. A., as quoted in S. Blanton, "The Power of Faith," in Peale and Blanton, *Faith Is the Answer,* 4.

59. For instance, her sentence "I haven't many *sins,* unless lack of faith is one" (1940 edition, 18) is silently altered in the 1955 edition to "I haven't *even any sins worth repenting,* unless lack of faith is one" (4; second emphasis added).

60. Rev. Arthur M. Tingue, Report of Executive Director to the Board of Directors, American Foundation of Religion and Psychiatry, November 5, 1964, IRH Papers; though odd-sounding, the sentence is cited correctly.

61. S. Blanton, "Dr. Freud for the Pulpit."

62. S. Blanton, *Diary,* 84, 86.

3
From Acute Shyness to "World Conquest"

1. See, for instance, Edward L. R. Elson, *America's Spiritual Recovery,* with an introduction by J. Edgar Hoover (Westwood, N.J.: Revell, 1954), especially chapter 4: "The Sickle or the Cross?" Elson was pastor to President Eisenhower and "to a congregation of Cabinet Members, Congressmen, and

other top government officials" at the National Presbyterian Church, Washington, D.C. (book jacket).

2. Examples include Edward F. Hutton, Westbury, N.Y., advertisement: "The Basic Issue Facing Us Today Is Just This: Americanism or Communism!" *New York Times*, July 14, 1947; also Hutton, "Help Rekindle Faith, Flaming Zeal in Our Constitution!" ad for the Committee for Constitutional Government, c. 1943, Norman Vincent Peale Papers, Special Collections Research Center, Syracuse University Libraries (hereafter "NVP papers"); and Peale to Hutton, July 21, 1947, NVP papers. All are discussed below.

3. Norman Vincent Peale, "Democracy Is the Child of Religion," October 10, 1948, 1–2, NVP papers.

4. A. Roy Eckardt, "The New Look in American Piety," *Christian Century* 17 (November 17, 1954), 1396.

5. "Peale Criticizes Alien Ideologies: Their Pressure Here Is Peril to the Sovereignty of Our Democracy, He Asserts," *New York Times*, May 30, 1938; "Labor Is Warned of 'Foreign' Taint. Peale Fears 'Red' Aspect of Agitation Is a Token of Un-American Trends. Deplores Bitter Spirit," *New York Times*, January 18, 1937.

6. "'Christ or Marx' Issue of Hour, Says Dr. Peale. U.S. Must Choose between Church and the Reds, He Declares in Sermon," *New York Herald Tribune*, January 20, 1936. Peale made this argument more than a decade before the publication of such ex-Marxist tracts as James Burnham, *The Coming Defeat of Communism* (New York: John Day, 1949). For details on party membership numbers, see Ellen Schrecker, "The American Communist Party," in *The Age of McCarthyism: A Brief History with Documents*, 2nd edition (New York: Bedford / St. Martin's, 2002), 7–8.

7. Carol V. R. George, *God's Salesman: Norman Vincent Peale and the Power of Positive Thinking* (New York: Oxford University Press, 1993), 15. For "God and gumption" the source is the mother of Governor A. Harry Moore, four-term governor of New Jersey and a friend of Peale's. She is quoted in the latter's autobiography: Norman Vincent Peale, *This Incredible Century* (Wheaton, Ill.: Living Books, 1991), 183.

8. "Dr. Peale Sees Faith as Source of Power," *New York American*, February 3, 1936; "Dr. Peale Sees Freedom and Faith Periled," *New York American*, February 15, 1937; "Christianity Seen in Race with Chaos. Final Destiny of Civilization in Our World Is the Prize, Dr. N. V. Peale Declares," *New York Times*, April 11, 1938.

9. Kevin M. Kruse, *One Nation under God: How Corporate America Invented Christian America* (New York: Basic Books, 2015), 5, 39.

10. "New Deal Assailed as Curb on Reform: Dr. Peale Charges Hasty

Moves for Selfish Ends Impede Real Social Progress. Ill-Conceived Experimentation Makes Public Wary of Progress, He Warns," *New York Times*, May 6, 1935.

11. "Peale Assails Class Conflict: Criticizes Methods Used by Roosevelt," *New York Sun*, January 13, 1936; "Dr. Peale Asks America to Put Roosevelt Out. Country Must Change Him or Change Constitution, He Declares in Sermon," *New York American*, June 1, 1936.

12. "Public Officials Require Watching, Pastor Warns . . . Criticizes Roosevelt's 'Indifference to Religion': Dr. Peale Calls It Cause of Vital New Deal Errors," *New York Herald Tribune*, August 19, 1935; "Dr. Peale Sees Freedom and Faith Periled"; "Peale Criticizes Alien Ideologies."

13. Peale, *This Incredible Century*, 127, xi.

14. Robert C. Murphy, "Think Right! Reverend Peale's Panacea," *The Nation*, May 7, 1955, 398.

15. George, *God's Salesman*, 129.

16. Ibid., 166.

17. Ibid., 176.

18. Edward Lodge Curran, *Spain in Arms: With Notes on Communism* (New York: American Committee against Communism, 1936); and Curran, *Facts about Communism* (Brooklyn, N.Y.: International Catholic Truth Society, 1937).

19. John Roy Carlson, *Under Cover* (New York: E. P. Dutton, 1943), 475.

20. Orville Prescott, "Books of the Times," *New York Times*, July 19, 1943.

21. Norman Vincent Peale to John Ray Carlson, September 27, 1943, NVP papers.

22. E. A. Rumely to Messrs. Gannett, Pettengill, Gerard, Williamson, Harding, March 10, 1943, NVP papers.

23. Hutton, advertisement, "The Basic Issue Facing Us Today."

24. Peale to Hutton, July 21, 1947.

25. Norman Vincent Peale to Helen K. Cleveland, April 21, 1954, NVP papers; Kruse, *One Nation under God*, 81.

26. Peale to Hutton, July 21, 1947. Peale's October 1948 sermon "Democracy Is the Child of Religion" clearly alludes to Rumely's phrase.

27. A longer, more detailed account of this history appears in Christopher Lane, *The Age of Doubt: Tracing the Roots of Our Religious Uncertainty* (New Haven: Yale University Press, 2011), 36–57.

28. Peale, "Democracy Is the Child of Religion," 2.

29. Peale to Hutton, July 21, 1947.

30. Dr. Dwight J. Bradley, National Citizens' Political Action Committee, in a letter about Peale to *Zion's Herald*, December 27, 1944, NVP papers.

31. Norman Vincent Peale to John Sutherland Bonnell, November 8, 1944, NVP papers. See also Peale to Ralph Sockman (then minister of Christ Church, Methodist, on Park Avenue, New York City), December 21, 1944, NVP papers.

32. Sermon Publication Committee, *Grassroots in Manhattan,* undated pamphlet of the Marble Collegiate Church, reprinted from the November 1943 issue of the *Christian Herald,* NVP papers.

33. Advertising Council, "Religion in American Life" campaign (1949), emphasis in original, as quoted in Kruse, *One Nation under God,* 132.

34. George, *God's Salesman,* 114; editorial in *Guideposts,* April 1948, as quoted in George, *God's Salesman,* 114.

35. Peale, fund-raising letter for the Foundation for Christian Living, January 1957, NVP papers.

36. George, *God's Salesman,* 129. See also Peale, *Perils to Freedom: A Sermon* (New York: Marble Collegiate Church, 1948); and Peale, *Preserving the American Tradition: A Thanksgiving Day Message* (New York: Marble Collegiate Church, 1948), both in NVP papers.

37. Peale on January 31, 1941, in a report on his views by the *New York American,* NVP papers.

38. Norman Vincent Peale to George E. Stringfellow, July 21, 1947, NVP papers.

39. "Church Seen Confusing Its Creed with Socialism: Dr. Peale Says Christ Did Not Oppose Capitalism," *New York Herald Tribune,* October 7, 1935.

40. Norman Vincent Peale, "Let the Church Speak Up for Capitalism," *Reader's Digest,* September 1950, 130.

41. Minutes, Joint Meeting—Members and Board Members, January 4, 1956, Institutes of Religion and Health Records, Special Collections Research Center, Syracuse University Libraries (hereafter "IRH papers").

42. *Gaining the Clergyman's Understanding: A Report of the Public Opinion Index for Industry* 9.8—351-D (Princeton, N.J.: Opinion Research Corporation, August 1951), NVP papers. Peale's copy is stamped "Confidential—Not for publication . . . for use of clients only."

43. Norman Vincent Peale, *The Coming of the King* (Englewood Cliffs, N.J.: Prentice Hall, 1956); Peale, *The Positive Power of Jesus Christ* (Pawling, N.Y.: FCL, 1980); Peale, *In God We Trust: A Positive Faith for Troubled Times* (Nashville, Tenn.: Thomas Nelson, 1994); and Peale, *Sin, Sex and Self-Control* (Carmel, N.Y.: Guideposts, 1965).

44. "Peale Traces Failure to Fear over Security," *New York Herald Tribune,* October 24, 1938.

45. Marx famously called religion an "opiate of the people" in his introduction to Karl Marx, *A Contribution to the Critique of Hegel's Philosophy of Right* (1843), published in *Deutsch-Französische Jahrbücher* in 1844.

46. See Norman M. Naimark, *Stalin's Genocides* (Princeton, N.J.: Princeton University Press, 2010); Frank Dikötter, *Mao's Great Famine: The History of China's Most Devastating Catastrophe, 1958–62* (New York: Walker, 2010).

47. Ira Katznelson, *Fear Itself: The New Deal and the Origins of Our Time* (New York: Liveright, 2013), 418, 95.

48. "Communism Destroys Individual, Says Peale. But Christianity Is Steadfast for 'Nobility of Man,'" *New York Herald Tribune*, September 14, 1936; also "Christianity Gives Man Important Place: Peale," *New York American*, September 14, 1936.

49. Peale, "Let the Church Speak Up for Capitalism," 128.

50. Norman Vincent Peale to Morton R. Cross, November 21, 1950, NVP papers.

51. Cross to Peale, November 22, 1950, NVP papers.

52. "Dr. Peale Warns Labor to Be Wary of Betrayal. 'Sit Down' Strike a Communist Import, He Declares," *New York Herald Tribune*, January 6, 1937; also, "Labor Is Warned of 'Foreign' Taint."

53. Norman Vincent Peale and Smiley Blanton, *Faith Is the Answer: A Pastor and a Psychiatrist Discuss Your Problems* (1940; Carmel, N.Y.: Guideposts, 1955), 45.

54. Peale, *This Incredible Century*, 24.

55. Ibid., 84, 80.

56. George, *God's Salesman*, 22, 21.

57. Norman Vincent Peale, 1932 speech before the Women's Christian Temperance Union convention in Syracuse, as quoted in George, *God's Salesman*, 64; "W.C.T.U. Plans Temperance by Education Campaign. Peale Assures Them That Prohibition Is Returning," *New York Herald Tribune*, January 16, 1937.

58. "Sensuality Viewed as Supreme Crime: Dr. Peale Warns against Decay of Qualities That Seek Lasting Beauty," *New York Times*, April 22, 1935.

59. Norman Vincent Peale, handwritten recollection, without pages or date (likely from 1958), quoted in George, *God's Salesman*, 52.

60. Peale, *This Incredible Century*, 66.

61. See, for instance, Alfred Adler, "Advantages and Disadvantages of the Inferiority Feeling" (1933), in Heinz L. Ansbacher and Rowena R. Ansbacher, eds., *Superiority and Social Interest: A Collection of Later Writings* (Evanston, Ill.: Northwestern University Press, 1970), 50–58.

62. Peale, *This Incredible Century*, 68, 66.

63. Ibid. 42.

64. Ibid., 36.

65. This doctrinal belief is discussed in Lane, *The Age of Doubt*, 76–77.

66. Peale, *This Incredible Century*, 37.

67. Ibid.

68. On its being a minor problem, see George, *God's Salesman*, citing a late interview with Peale: "In fact, he said, as with a person recovering from alcoholism, it was a problem that never really left him" (26).

69. Peale, *This Incredible Century*, 129.

70. Ibid., 126–28.

71. "Dr. Peale Sees Freedom and Faith Periled"; Peale, *This Incredible Century*, 137–38.

72. "Research—1. In Religion and Psychiatry," document attached to a letter from John M. Cotton to Dr. Bernard Barber, February 13, 1959, IRH papers.

73. George, *God's Salesman*, 38.

74. One of Peale's listeners and early clients, as quoted in Peale, *This Incredible Century*, 41.

75. Ibid., 81: "I have since eschewed politics," Peale writes in 1991 about his autobiographical chapter on the 1920s, "and I think a minister should never take a partisan stand unless some moral issue is involved. He is bound to hurt his spiritual ministry if he is considered 'political.'" That did not stop him from later arguing that John F. Kennedy's Catholicism would make him ineligible for office, since his loyalties (to Washington and to Rome) allegedly would be divided.

76. "Enthusiasm Need for Conquest of Christian World," *Syracuse Post-Standard*, July 2, 1928.

4

The Peale-Hoover-Eisenhower Empire

1. "Church Warned to Go Modern If It Would Live: Dr. Peale Suggests Turning to Radio and Films to Revive Lay Interest," *New York Herald Tribune*, April 29, 1935.

2. Norman Vincent Peale, "Formula for Efficiency," *NBC Network*, February 18, 1951; "Science of a Satisfying Life," *NBC Network*, December 9, 1951; "Faith Attitude Overcomes Every Difficulty," *NBC Network*, November 18, 1951; and "How to Be Reborn, or What Is Personal Resurrection?" *Guideposts*, April 1955, all in Norman Vincent Peale Papers, Special Col-

lections Research Center, Syracuse University Libraries (hereafter "NVP papers").

3. Norman Vincent Peale, *The Power of Positive Thinking* (1952; New York: Fireside, 2003), 1, 44.

4. Reinhold Niebuhr, "Varieties of Religious Revival," *New Republic*, June 6, 1955, 13. See also Curtis Cate, "God and Success," *Atlantic Monthly*, April 1957, 74–76.

5. Norman Vincent Peale, *This Incredible Century* (Wheaton, Ill.: Living Books, 1991), 201.

6. Peale, *The Power of Positive Thinking*, 5. The Bible passage repeats on pp. 43, 86, and 91.

7. Ibid., 5.

8. Ibid., 163.

9. Norman Vincent Peale, "Faith Attitude Overcomes Every Difficulty," *NBC Network*, November 18, 1951, 2.

10. The main promoter of the term was Peale's ally James Fifield, quoted here in *The Defender*, August 1944, 13, NVP papers. The term was also taken up by the conservative group Spiritual Mobilization, on whose board Peale served from 1944.

11. Peale, *The Power of Positive Thinking*, 163, 127; Bruce Barton, *The Man Nobody Knows: A Discovery of the Real Jesus* (New York: Grosset and Dunlap, 1925); Oral Roberts and G. H. Montgomery, eds., *God's Formula for Success and Prosperity* (Tulsa, Okla.: Oral Roberts, 1955).

12. Peale, *This Incredible Century*, 198–99.

13. Peale, as quoted in "Peale Comes Home, Certain Country's Dry," *Syracuse Post-Standard*, September 20, 1931.

14. Rev. Harry C. Meserve (then minister of the First Unitarian Church of San Francisco), "The New Piety," *Atlantic Monthly*, June 1955, 35.

15. See, for instance, Roberts and Montgomery, *God's Formula for Success and Prosperity*.

16. J. Ronald Oakley, *God's Country: America in the Fifties* (New York: Barricade, 1986), 323.

17. For "vogue": Niebuhr, "Varieties of Religious Revival," 13; "fad": Canon Bernard Iddings Bell, quoted in Paul Hutchinson, "Have We a 'New' Religion?" *Life*, April 11, 1955, 157.

18. Peale, *This Incredible Century*, 198.

19. Hutchinson, "Have We a 'New' Religion?" 148.

20. Ibid., 150, 148.

21. Carol V. R. George, *God's Salesman: Norman Vincent Peale and the Power of Positive Thinking* (New York: Oxford University Press, 1993), 130.

22. "Of the Millions Who Live—Only a Few Are Remembered!" Un-dated promotional brochure for the American Foundation of Religion and Psychiatry (1960s), Institutes of Religion and Health Records, Special Collections Research Center, Syracuse University Libraries (hereafter "IRH papers").

23. Norman Vincent Peale with Elmer Hess, M.D., president of the American Medical Association, *Medicine's Proclamation of Faith* (Atlantic City, N.J., June 7, 1955); "religious healing" and "religiously motivated ideas": from "Research—1. In Religion and Psychiatry," document attached to a letter from John M. Cotton to Dr. Bernard Barber, February 13, 1959; both brochure and document are in IRH papers.

24. Peale, *This Incredible Century*, 180–81.

25. Oakley, *God's Country*, 323–24.

26. Hutchinson, "Have We a 'New' Religion?" 157.

27. Peale, *The Power of Positive Thinking*, 151.

28. Ibid., 107.

29. For more on the history of such religious broadcasts, see David Edwin Harrell, Jr., "Pentecost at Prime Time," *Christian History* 15 (1996), 52–54.

30. Norman Vincent Peale, *Stay Alive All Your Life* (1957; New York: Fireside, 2003), 256.

31. Peale, *The Power of Positive Thinking*, 167, 34.

32. George, *God's Salesman*, 31. For more on such associations in Peale's writing, see his *Sin, Sex and Self-Control: A Practical, Common-Sense, Inspiring Challenge to the Individual* (Carmen, N.Y.: Guideposts, 1965). The book, according to its jacket, "explores the collapse of moral standards and how to reverse [the] dangerous trend in family life, business, politics, education and even church. Dr. Peale's forthright message is that God is offering us a magnificent new maturity."

33. William Lee Miller, *Piety along the Potomac: Notes on Politics and Morals in the '50s* (Boston: Houghton Mifflin, 1964), 134–35. (Miller's article on Peale was first published in *The Reporter*, January 13, 1955, 19–24.)

34. Donald Meyer, "Confidence Man," *New Republic*, July 11, 1955, 8–10.

35. Miller, *Piety along the Potomac*, 139, 138.

36. Albert Ellis, psychologist and founder of cognitive theory, *Overcoming Resistance: Rational-Emotive Therapy with Difficult Clients* (New York: Springer, 1985), 147.

37. Robert C. Murphy, "Think Right! Reverend Peale's Panacea," *The Nation*, May 7, 1955, 399.

38. For "syrupy": ibid.; William Peters, "The Case against 'Easy' Religion,"

Redbook, September 1955, 93. See also Barbara Ehrenreich, *Bright-Sided: How Positive Thinking Is Undermining America* (New York: Picador, 2010), 92–93.

39. Edmund Fuller, "Pitchmen in the Pulpit," *Saturday Review,* March 9, 1957, 28.

40. George, *God's Salesman,* 141.

41. See, for instance, Karl Menninger, M.D., "Psychiatry," in Harold E. Stearns, ed., *America Now: An Inquiry into Civilization in the United States* (New York: Scribner's, 1938), especially 450–53 ("The Influence of Psychiatry upon Religion"); and Menninger, foreword to Robert G. Gassert and Bernard H. Hall, *Psychiatry and Religious Faith* (New York: Viking Press, 1964), xiii–xiv. The cultural impact of the first *Diagnostic and Statistical Manual of Mental Disorders (DSM),* published in 1952 by the American Psychiatric Association, is assessed in my next chapter.

42. Proposed constitutional amendment introduced by Senator Ralph Flanders, quoted in Albert G. Huegli, ed., *Church and State under God* (St. Louis: Concordia, 1964), 429.

43. The event in New York City resulted mostly in reconversions. At least 60 percent of the event's "decisions for Christ" were by those already committed to a church: "A Mighty City Hears Billy's Mighty Call," *Life,* May 27, 1957, 25.

44. Prayer card (1952), as quoted in Kevin M. Kruse, *One Nation under God: How Corporate America Invented Christian America* (New York: Basic Books, 2015), 54.

45. Donald Meyer, *The Positive Thinkers: A Study of the American Quest for Health, Wealth and Personal Power from Mary Baker Eddy to Norman Vincent Peale* (New York: Doubleday, 1965), 259–68.

46. Miller, *Piety along the Potomac,* jacket blurb.

47. I am grateful to one of the readers for Yale University Press for helping me formulate this point.

48. Peale, *Stay Alive All Your Life,* 252.

49. George, *God's Salesman,* 63.

50. Smiley Blanton, *Love or Perish* (1955; New York: Fawcett Crest, 1956), 99, 149.

51. Norman Vincent Peale, "The Hidden Energies of the Mind," in Peale and Smiley Blanton, *Faith Is the Answer: A Pastor and a Psychiatrist Discuss Your Problems* (1940; Carmel, N.Y.: Guideposts, 1955), 48.

52. Smiley Blanton to Norman Vincent Peale, October 21, 1949, NVP papers. His other recommended books were William Menninger and Munro

Leaf, *You and Psychiatry* (New York: Scribner's, 1948); and Helen Flanders Dunbar, *Mind and Body: Psychosomatic Medicine* (New York: Random House, 1947).

53. Sigmund Freud to Rev. Oskar Pfister, November 25, 1928, in Sigmund Freud, *Psychoanalysis and Faith: Dialogues with the Reverend Oskar Pfister*, ed. Heinrich Meng and Ernst L. Freud, trans. Eric Mosbacher (New York: Basic Books, 1963), 126.

54. A. Roy Eckardt, *The Surge of Piety in America: An Appraisal* (New York: Association Press, 1958). In *Religious History of the American People* (New Haven: Yale University Press, 1972), Sydney Ahlstrom determined from an array of data that 1958 was the high point for religious attendance and that by 1959 "discerning observers began talking about the postwar revival in the past tense" (962).

55. See, for instance, Stephanie Muravchik, "The Rise and Fall of Psychoreligious Cooperation," in *American Protestantism in the Age of Psychology* (New York: Cambridge University Press, 2011), 1–24; and, more broadly, E. Brooks Holifield, *A History of Pastoral Care in America: From Salvation to Self-Realization* (Nashville, Tenn.: Abingdon Press, 1983); and Holifield, *Health and Medicine in the Methodist Tradition: Journey toward Wholeness* (New York: Crossroad, 1986).

56. Peale, *This Incredible Century*, 144.

57. Norman Vincent Peale, "The Magic of Believing," January 7, 1951; "Formula for Eliminating Worry," January 21, 1951, both the text of radio addresses, NVP papers; and, Peale with Smiley Blanton, "Are You Looking for God?" *American Magazine*, October 1947.

58. Peale, *This Incredible Century*, 144.

59. Ibid., 142–43.

60. Robert D. Putnam and David E. Campbell, *American Grace: How Religion Divides and Unites Us* (New York: Simon and Schuster, 2010), 84.

61. J. Edgar Hoover, introduction to Edward L. R. Elson, *America's Spiritual Recovery* (Westwood, N.J.: Revell, 1954), 10.

62. J. Edgar Hoover, "Parents Are Not Enough," *Guideposts* 1.7 (September 1947), emphasis in original.

63. "Ike Says Faith Keeps Him Going: He'd Crack without It," *New York World-Telegram and Sun*, November 8, 1957; Norman Vincent Peale, as quoted in "Eisenhower Calls Faith His Shield: Saves Him from Mental Hospital," undated newspaper clipping in NVP papers.

64. Eisenhower, remarks of the president for "Back to God" program, February 20, 1955, as quoted in Kruse, *One Nation under God*, 75.

65. Norman Vincent Peale to J. Edgar Hoover, December 20, 1956, NVP papers.

66. Hoover to Peale, March 18, 1958, NVP papers.

67. Peale to Hoover, April 22, 1958, NVP papers.

68. Hoover to Peale, March 13, 1959, NVP papers.

69. Other high-profile names featured were Faith Baldwin, Ben Hogan, Jane Froman, and Fred Waring (Hutchinson, "Have We a 'New' Religion?" 157). Peale went on to officiate at the marriage of Eisenhower's grandson, Dwight David Eisenhower II, to Julie Nixon (the incoming president's younger daughter) on December 22, 1968, just weeks after Richard Nixon had won the presidency; see Doug Wead, *All the Presidents' Children: Triumph and Tragedy in the Lives of America's First Families* (New York: Atria, 2003), 252.

70. Kruse, *One Nation under God*, 74.

71. Dwight D. Eisenhower, "Remarks by the President at the Graduation Exercises of the FBI National Academy in the Departmental Auditorium," November 8, 1957, NVP papers. See also "Peale, President Address FBI Class," *Washington Post and Times Herald*, November 9, 1957.

72. Norman Vincent Peale to General Douglas MacArthur, April 11, 1958, NVP papers.

73. The Republican National Committee, as quoted in Douglas T. Miller and Marion Nowak, *The Fifties: The Way We Really Were* (Garden City, N.Y.: Doubleday, 1977), 90. See also Herbert H. Hyman and Paul B. Sheatsley, "The Political Appeal of President Eisenhower," *Public Opinion Quarterly* 17.4 (1953–54): "the issues of Communism, corruption, and Korea, over which the 1952 campaign was fought, were of decidedly less importance than was the simple candidacy of Dwight D. Eisenhower" (460).

74. Eisenhower to press secretary Jim Hagerty, recalled in an April 17, 1968, interview with Ed Edwin for a Columbia University Oral History Project, as quoted in Kruse, *One Nation under God*, 73.

75. Kruse, *One Nation under God*, 73.

76. Oakley, *God's Country*, 320. Eisenhower, as quoted in Miller, *Piety along the Potomac*, 21.

77. Miller, *Piety along the Potomac*, 19.

78. Eisenhower, as quoted in Miller, *Piety along the Potomac*, 20; Stanley Hugh, "What the President Wants," *Reader's Digest*, April 1953, 2, 4.

79. Miller, *Piety along the Potomac*, 18–19, 33, 21.

80. Arthur Schlesinger, Jr., described the transformation in "When Patriotism Wasn't Religious," *New York Times*, July 7, 2002.

81. Oakley, *God's Country,* 320.

82. Elson, *America's Spiritual Recovery,* 48–49, 53.

83. Miller and Nowak, *The Fifties: The Way We Really Were,* 90.

84. Eisenhower, as quoted in Miller, *Piety along the Potomac,* 45–46.

85. Miller, *Piety along the Potomac,* 44, 20.

86. Oakley, *God's Country,* 319. See also Jon Butler, *Awash in a Sea of Faith: Christianizing the American People* (Cambridge, Mass.: Harvard University Press, 1990); and Charles H. Lippy, *Being Religious, American Style: A History of Popular Religiosity in the United States* (Westport, Conn.: Praeger, 1994), chapters 7 and 8.

87. Miller, *Piety along the Potomac,* 127. An example of a feature article is "The New Evangelist" (on Graham), *Time,* October 25, 1954.

5
Psychiatry Goes to Church

1. Paul Hutchinson, "Have We a 'New' Religion?" *Life,* April 11, 1955, 151, 150.

2. Smiley Blanton to Norman Vincent Peale, March 1, 1950. On April 4 of the same year, he reiterated to Peale, "As a result of your speaking and [books], we have increased calls for the services of the clinic." Both communications are in Norman Vincent Peale Papers, Special Collections Research Center, Syracuse University Libraries (hereafter "NVP papers").

3. Claire Cox, director of public relations, "Suggested Public Relations Policies," updated November 12, 1965; and Cox, "Guidelines for Speechmakers," updated April 1966, 3, both in Institutes of Religion and Health Records, Special Collections Research Center, Syracuse University Libraries (hereafter "IRH papers").

4. Confidential minutes of Administrative Meeting, November 27, 1960, IRH papers.

5. Iago Galdston, M.D., to Smiley Blanton, December 29, 1955, IRH papers.

6. Samuel Z. Klausner, *Psychiatry and Religion: A Sociological Study of the New Alliance of Ministers and Psychiatrists* (Glencoe, Ill.: Free Press, 1964), vii.

7. Iago Galdston, M.D., to Dr. Howard M. LeSourd, November 8, 1956, IRH papers.

8. See, for instance, E. Brooks Holifield, *A History of Pastoral Care in America: From Salvation to Self-Realization* (Nashville, Tenn.: Abingdon

Press, 1983), chapter 6; Stephanie Muravchik, *American Protestantism in the Age of Psychology* (New York: Cambridge University Press, 2011), chapters 1 and 2; and Rebecca L. Davis, *More Perfect Unions: The American Search for Marital Bliss* (Cambridge, Mass.: Harvard University Press, 2010), chapter 5, which, with Muravchik's book, describes a world of "psychological testing" by clergymen counseling married couples.

9. Hugh S. Hostetler to Smiley Blanton, January 26, 1963, IRH papers. Blanton's two-page reply is similarly heated: "If you tell a person he is a quack, incompetent, and a knave, it is a good deal more than just being 'severe and austere.' It is a vicious attack on a person's character and ability" (February 2, 1963, IRH papers).

10. Hutchinson, "Have We a 'New' Religion?" 157, 144.

11. Norman Vincent Peale and Smiley Blanton, "Are You Looking for God?" *American Magazine*, October 1947, 21; American Foundation of Religion and Psychiatry, "Of the Millions Who Live—Only a Few Are Remembered!" undated promotional brochure from the 1960s, IRH papers.

12. *How Religion and Psychiatry Work Together: Facts about the American Foundation of Religion and Psychiatry*, brochure (post-1963), IRH papers.

13. Clinic staff member Dr. Nielson, as quoted in Klausner, *Psychiatry and Religion*, 227.

14. Clinic staff member Dr. Norton, as quoted in Klausner, *Psychiatry and Religion*, 233. See also Joshua Loth Liebman, *Peace of Mind* (New York: Simon and Schuster, 1946), especially chapter 9: "Where Religion and Psychology Part—and Meet"; and Andrew R. Heinze, "*Peace of Mind* (1946): Judaism and the Therapeutic Polemics of Postwar America," *Religion and American Culture* 12.1 (2002), 31–58.

15. Additionally, Iago Galdston's collection *Freud in Contemporary Culture* (New York: International Universities Press, 1957) included chapters titled "Freud and Medicine," "Freud and Psychiatry," "Freud and Prophylaxis," and "Freud in the Perspective of Medical History."

16. Galdston to LeSourd, November 8, 1956.

17. Norman Vincent Peale to Smiley Blanton, June 22, 1955, IRH papers.

18. Samuel Z. Klausner, as quoted in minutes of Sixth Annual Meeting of Board of Governors, October 5, 1959, 4, IRH papers. In addition to *Psychiatry and Religion*, Klausner's published works include "The Religio-Psychiatric Movement (Lecture I)," *Review of Religious Research* 5.2 (1964), 63–74; and "The Religio-Psychiatric Movement: Changing Ideology of the Movement (Lecture II)," *Review of Religious Research* 6.1 (1964), 7–22.

19. Mrs. Arthur H. Kukner to Dr. and Mrs. Peale (board members copied), October 28, 1958, IRH papers.

20. Minutes, Joint meeting—Members and Board Members, January 4, 1956, IRH papers.

21. Minutes of Sixth Annual Meeting of Board of Governors, October 5, 1959, 3.

22. Confidential minutes, November 27, 1960, 4.

23. Douglas T. Miller and Marion Nowak, *The Fifties: The Way We Really Were* (Garden City, N.Y.: Doubleday, 1977), 138; Mickey C. Smith, *A Social History of the Minor Tranquilizers: The Quest for Small Comfort in the Age of Anxiety* (Binghamton, N.Y.: Pharmaceutical Products Press, 1991).

24. American Psychiatric Association, *Diagnostic and Statistical Manual of Mental Disorders* (Washington, D.C.: APA, 1952).

25. Ibid., 35, 37.

26. Stefan A. Pasternak, "The Explosive, Antisocial, and Passive-Aggressive Personalities," in John R. Lion, ed., *Personality Disorders: Diagnosis and Management* (Baltimore: Williams and Wilkins, 1974), 63.

27. For "empire Psychotropia": Anne E. Caldwell, "History of Psychopharmacology," in William G. Clark and Joseph del Guidice, eds., *Principles of Psychopharmacology,* 2nd edition (New York: Academic Press, 1978), 35; descriptions: Smith, *A Social History of the Minor Tranquilizers,* 67.

28. Smiley Blanton to "research departments of pharmaceutical companies," attachment to letter from Kukner to Dr. and Mrs. Peale, October 28, 1958.

29. Ibid. Other pharmaceutical companies that were approached include Ayerst Labs; Hoffmann-Laroche; Lederle Laboratories; Parke, Davis, and Co.; G. D. Searle and Co.; Smith, Kline and French; Squibb and Sons; and Wallace Laboratories. The IRH papers unfortunately do not include their responses.

30. "Very Confidential" minutes of Administrative Meeting, November 4, 1958, IRH papers.

31. See, for instance, Smiley Blanton to David L. Sills, Acting Director, Bureau of Applied Social Research, January 14, 1960, IRH papers.

32. Minutes of Administrative Committee Meeting, July 5, 1966, IRH papers.

33. Minutes of Annual Meeting of Board of Directors, November 12, 1968, 3, IRH papers.

34. Rev. Arthur M. Tingue, Report of Executive Director to the Board of Directors, May 4, 1966, 3, IRH papers.

35. "Research—1. In Religion and Psychiatry," attachment to letter from John M. Cotton to Dr. Bernard Barber, February 13, 1959, IRH papers.

36. "A Program of Research in Prevention and Early Detection of Mental

Illness," attachment to Rev. Arther M. Tingue, Report of Executive Director to the Board of Directors, American Foundation of Religion and Psychiatry, November 5, 1964, IRH papers.

37. "A Program to Relate the Work of the Foundation to the Needs of Executives and Corporations," attachment to Tingue, Report of Executive Director to the Board of Directors, November 5, 1964.

38. Minutes, Board of Directors Meeting, April 5, 1965, IRH papers.

39. "A Program to Relate the Work of the Foundation to the Needs of National Religious Leaders," attachment to Tingue, Report of Executive Director to the Board of Directors, November 5, 1964.

40. Klausner, *Psychiatry and Religion*, 201–2.

41. Ibid., 221–22n6.

42. Ibid.

43. Ibid., 202.

44. David L. Sills to Drs. Blanton, Cotton, and LeSourd, "Progress of Research," May 5, 1959, 2; Samuel Z. Klausner to Smiley Blanton, "Progress Report, Fall 1957," January 15, 1958, 1, both in IRH papers.

45. Charles K. Glock, Director of Bureau of Applied Social Research, Columbia University, to Smiley Blanton, November 27, 1956, IRH papers.

46. Klausner, *Psychiatry and Religion*, 201.

47. "A Proposal for Research into Some of the Problems Bearing on Current Efforts to Integrate Religion and Psychiatry in Combating Mental and Emotional Diseases," submitted to Rockefeller Brothers Fund February 12, 1957, IRH papers.

48. Charles K. Glock, "The Descriptive Phase," planned research schedule attachment to November 27, 1956, letter to Smiley Blanton, 1–2, IRH papers.

49. Klausner, *Psychiatry and Religion*, viii.

50. Report of Executive Director of Executive Committee, September 30, 1963, 2, IRH papers.

51. Samuel Z. Klausner to Smiley Blanton, February 18, 1962, IRH papers.

52. Dr. Nielsen, as quoted in Klausner, *Psychiatry and Religion*, 234.

53. Dr. Lyman and Mr. Youngs, as quoted in Klausner, *Psychiatry and Religion*, 249.

54. Ronald Bayer, *Homosexuality and American Psychiatry: The Politics of Diagnosis* (New York: Basic Books, 1981).

55. Klausner, "The Religio-Psychiatric Movement (Lecture I)," 65.

56. Samuel Z. Klausner, "The Mellowing of the Religio-Psychiatric Movement," conference paper from June 13–14, 1963, IRH papers, parts of which appear in Klausner, "The Religio-Psychiatric Movement (Lecture II)," 22.

57. Author interview with Nunzio Gubitosa, Jane Roberts, and Nancy Moore Simpson, senior administrators at Blanton-Peale Institute and Counseling Center, New York City, July 12, 2013.

58. Klausner, "The Religio-Psychiatric Movement (Lecture II)," 22.

59. Klausner, *Psychiatry and Religion*, 12, 32–33.

60. Ibid., 33, 32.

61. Ibid., 1.

62. Ibid., 257–66.

63. Clifton E. Kew (head psychologist at Religio-Psychiatric Clinic) and Clinton J. Kew, "Psychiatry Goes to Church," *Why? The Magazine of Popular Psychology*, January 1952; Hector J. Ritey, M.D., "The Common Grounds between Psychiatry and Religion," *Mental Hygiene* 48.3 (July 1964), 351–55.

64. Elmer Hess, M.D., president of American Medical Association, and Norman Vincent Peale, *Medicine's Proclamation of Faith* (Atlantic City, N.J., June 7, 1955), 17, IRH papers.

65. Group for the Advancement of Psychiatry, *Psychiatry and Religion: Some Steps toward Mutual Understanding and Usefulness, Formulated by Committee on Psychiatry and Religion* (New York: GAP, 1960); and, more recently, Lillian H. Robinson, ed., *Psychiatry and Religion: Overlapping Concerns* (New York: American Psychiatric Press, 1986).

66. Karl Menninger, M.D., foreword to Robert G. Gassert and Bernard H. Hall, *Psychiatry and Religious Faith* (New York: Viking Press, 1964), xiv. In 1956, Menninger served briefly on the Board of Directors of the American Foundation of Religion and Psychiatry, IRH papers.

67. Rev. Arthur M. Tingue, minutes of Board of Governors Meeting, October 1, 1962, 5, IRH papers.

68. Norman Vincent Peale to Dr. Grayson Kirk, president, Columbia University, December 14, 1961, IRH papers.

69. Dr. Bernard Berelson, director of Bureau of Applied Research, to W. M. Smith, vice president of the foundation, December 7, 1960, as quoted in Peale to Kirk, December 14, 1961.

70. Peale to Kirk, December 14, 1961.

71. Kirk to Peale, January 17, 1962, IRH papers.

72. See, for instance, Sydney Ahlstrom, *A Religious History of the American People* (New Haven: Yale University Press, 1972), 962; A. Roy Eckardt, *The Surge of Piety in America: An Appraisal* (New York: Association Press, 1958); and Klausner, "The Religio-Psychiatric Movement (Lecture I)," 64, which dates the peak of the revival to one year earlier, 1957.

73. The White House meeting took place on March 4, 1964, and concerned, in part, the role of religion in treating "mental retardation" and en-

suring mental health, as reported in minutes, Rev. Arthur M. Tingue to Executive Committee, March 4, 1964; on global expansion see minutes, Board of Directors Meeting, May 4, 1966, 4; both minutes are in IRH papers.

74. W. Clement Stone, as quoted in Report of Vice-President of Development to Board of Directors, October 4, 1965, IRH papers.

75. Douglas Martin, "Clement Stone Dies at 100; Built Empire on Optimism," *New York Times,* September 5, 2002.

76. Minutes, Rev. Arthur M. Tingue to Administrative Committee, March 2, 1965, IRH papers.

77. Cox, "Suggested Public Relations Policies," updated November 12, 1965.

6
Religion and Mental Health Rebalanced

1. Eric F. Goldman, "Good-by to the 'Fifties—and Good Riddance," *Harper's Magazine,* January 1960, 27, 28.

2. Arthur Godfrey, as quoted in Goldman, "Good-by to the 'Fifties," 29.

3. Norman Vincent Peale, *The Power of Positive Thinking* (1952; New York: Fireside, 2003), 174. The argument that religion is akin to a science has a long history in the United States; see, for instance, Andrew Dickson White, *A History of the Warfare of Science with Theology in Christendom* (1896; New York: Appleton, 1922).

4. Goldman, "Good-by to the 'Fifties," 28, 29.

5. Gordon W. Allport, *The Individual and His Religion: A Psychological Interpretation* (New York: Macmillan, 1950), 2.

6. Kenneth E. Appel, "Academy of Religion and Mental Health: Past and Future," *Journal of Religion and Health* 4.3 (1965), 210.

7. Goldman, "Good-by to the 'Fifties," 29.

8. "Science Isn't God," newspaper editorial, as quoted in Gordon W. Allport, "Behavioral Science, Religion, and Mental Health," *Journal of Religion and Health* 2.3 (April 1963), 196.

9. Ibid.

10. Institute on Religion in an Age of Science, Tenth Summer Conference, Star Island, off Portsmouth, N.H., July 27–August 3, 1963.

11. Ibid. See also Institute on Religion in an Age of Science, *Ten-Year View: 1953–1963* (Brookline, Mass., 1963).

12. Allport, "Behavioral Science, Religion, and Mental Health," 187. Additional representative publications include Group for the Advancement of

Psychiatry, *Psychiatry and Religion: Some Steps toward Mutual Understanding and Usefulness,* Report no. 48 (New York: GAP, 1960); O. Hobart Mowrer, "Psychiatry and Religion: The Rediscovery of Moral Responsibility," *The Atlantic,* July 1961, 88–92; Sue W. Spencer, "What Place Has Religion in Social Work Education?" *Social Service Review* 35.2 (June 1961), 161–70; Morton King, "Measuring the Religious Variable: Nine Proposed Dimensions," *Journal for the Scientific Study of Religion* 6.2 (Autumn 1967), 173–90; and Ralph Wendell Burhoe, "Bridging the Gap between Psychiatry and Theology," *Journal of Religion and Health* 7.3 (July 1968), 215–26.

13. Allport, *The Individual and His Religion,* 79; also Rev. Dr. Hans Hofmann, as quoted in Academy of Religion and Mental Health, *Religion, Science, and Mental Health: Proceedings of the First Academy Symposium on Inter-discipline Responsibility for Mental Health—A Religious and Scientific Concern, 1957* (New York: New York University Press, 1959), 55–57; and the comprehensive data that Robert D. Putnam and David E. Campbell present in *American Grace: How Religion Divides and Unites Us* (New York: Simon and Schuster, 2010), 100–106. On the search for consilience more broadly, see Ian Barbour, *Religion in an Age of Science* (New York: HarperCollins, 1990); E. O. Wilson, *In Search of Nature* (Washington, D.C.: Island Press, 1996); and Stephen Jay Gould, *Rocks of Ages: Science and Religion in the Fullness of Life* (New York: Ballantine, 1999), 47–96.

14. Harvey J. Tompkins et al., "Epilogue," in Academy of Religion and Mental Health, *Religion, Science, and Mental Health,* 101.

15. See Kevin M. Kruse, *One Nation under God: How Corporate America Invented Christian America* (New York: Basic Books, 2015), chapters 6–8; and Jonathan P. Herzog, *The Spiritual-Industrial Complex: America's Religious Battle against Communism in the Early Cold War* (New York: Oxford University Press, 2011), chapters 6 and 7.

16. Putnam and Campbell, *American Grace,* 98.

17. Ibid., 100.

18. Summary, Crook-Heritage Associates Possibility Study on Merger, attached to minutes of the Annual Meeting of the Board of Directors (W. Clement Stone presiding), November 12, 1968, Institutes of Religion and Health Records, Special Collections Research Center, Syracuse University Libraries (hereafter "IRH papers").

19. "A Vignette of the Academy," attached to minutes of Board of Directors meeting, April 1, 1971, 5, IRH papers.

20. Seward Hiltner, "An Appraisal of Religion and Psychiatry since 1954," *Journal of Religion and Health* 4.3 (1965), 222.

21. Appel, "Academy of Religion and Mental Health," 212.

22. George Christian Anderson, "Comprehensive Man" (1954), as quoted in Appel, "Academy of Religion and Mental Health," 208.

23. Ibid., 209.

24. George Christian Anderson, "The Partnership of Theologians and Psychiatrists," *Journal of Religion and Health* 3.1 (1963), 58; Anderson, as quoted in Appel, "Academy of Religion and Mental Health," 208.

25. Anderson, "The Partnership of Theologians and Psychiatrists," 63.

26. David E. Roberts, "Health from the Standpoint of the Christian Faith," in Paul B. Maves, ed., *The Church and Mental Health* (New York: Scribner's, 1953), 23, as quoted in Anderson, "The Partnership of Theologians and Psychiatrists," 62–63.

27. Anderson, "The Partnership of Theologians and Psychiatrists," 64.

28. Allport, *The Individual and His Religion,* 139.

29. Ibid., 24; Academy of Religion and Mental Health, *Religion, Science, and Mental Health,* 47; Anderson, "The Partnership of Theologians and Psychiatrists," 59–60.

30. Anderson, "The Partnership of Theologians and Psychiatrists," 60.

31. Gordon W. Allport, "Religion and Prejudice," chapter 28 of *The Nature of Prejudice* (New York: Anchor, 1954); and Allport, *The Individual and His Religion,* 64–65, 67.

32. Gregory Zilboorg, as quoted in Academy of Religion and Mental Health, *Religion, Science, and Mental Health,* 31.

33. Tompkins et al., "Epilogue," 101.

34. Ibid., 102–3.

35. Rev. Dr. Hans Hofmann, as quoted in Tompkins et al., "Epilogue," 54.

36. An unidentified clergyman, as quoted in Tompkins et al., "Epilogue," 46–47.

37. Ibid., 47. Subsequent research points to a decidedly more mixed picture, with results concerning psychological health frequently in religion's favor. For a comprehensive overview of such studies, see Harold G. Koenig, Michael E. McCullough, and Donald B. Larson, *Handbook of Religion and Health,* 2nd edition (Oxford: Oxford University Press, 2012), esp. part 3: "Research on Religion and Mental Health."

38. Rev. Dr. Hofmann, as quoted in Academy of Religion and Mental Health, *Religion, Science, and Mental Health,* 58.

39. An unidentified psychiatrist, as quoted in Academy of Religion and Mental Health, *Religion, Science, and Mental Health,* 94.

40. Otto Klineberg et al., eds., *Religion in the Developing Personality: Proceedings of the Second Academy Symposium, 1958* (New York: New York University Press, 1960).

41. An unidentified Protestant clergyman, as quoted in Academy of Religion and Mental Health, *Religion, Science, and Mental Health,* 95.

42. Roberts, "Health from the Standpoint of the Christian Faith," 23.

43. Dr. Earl A. Loomis, Jr., director of the Program in Psychiatry and Religion at Union Theological Seminary, as quoted in Academy of Religion and Mental Health, *Religion, Science, and Mental Health,* 90.

44. Appel, "Academy of Religion and Mental Health," 214, 213.

45. Justice Tom Clark, decision on *Abington School District v. Schempp,* 374 U.S. 203 (1963), June 17, 1963, as quoted in Kruse, *One Nation under God,* 198.

46. "List of Selections from the Standard American Version of the Bible" [1950s], handbook, Department of Education, State of Idaho; and Pennsylvania statute for public schools (1949), both quoted in Kruse, *One Nation under God,* 191, 192.

47. Norman Vincent Peale, as quoted in "Nixon Hopes Religious Rites Will Inspire Youth," *New York Times,* April 28, 1969. See also Andrew Preston (referring to the 1960s), in "The Revolutionary Church in a Revolutionary Age," in *Sword of the Spirit, Shield of Faith: Religion in American War and Diplomacy* (New York: Anchor Books, 2012), 501–19.

48. Anderson, "The Partnership of Theologians and Psychiatrists," 64.

49. Rev. Dr. Hofmann, as quoted in Academy of Religion and Mental Health, *Religion, Science, and Mental Health,* 54.

50. Rev. Noël Mailloux, as quoted in Academy of Religion and Mental Health, *Religion, Science, and Mental Health,* 64–65.

51. Rev. Dr. Hans Hofmann, as quoted in Academy of Religion and Mental Health, *Religion, Science, and Mental Health,* 55. See also his later essay, "Religion and Mental Health," *Journal of Religion and Health* 1.4 (July 1962), 319–36.

52. Rabbi Albert A. Goldman, as quoted in Academy of Religion and Mental Health, *Religion, Science, and Mental Health,* 83.

53. An unnamed medical educator, as quoted in Academy of Religion and Mental Health, *Religion, Science, and Mental Health,* 92.

54. An unnamed Catholic priest, as quoted in Academy of Religion and Mental Health, *Religion, Science, and Mental Health,* 93.

55. Hiltner, "An Appraisal of Religion and Psychiatry since 1954," 219. That emphasis is continuing under Pope Francis. See, for instance, Travis Gettys, "'God Is Not a Magician': Pope Says Christians Should Believe in Evolution and Big Bang," *Raw Story,* October 28, 2014, http://www.rawstory.com/rs/2014/10/god-is-not-a-magician-pope-says-christians-should-believe-in-evolution-and-big-bang/.

56. Archbishop Fulton J. Sheen, *Psychology and Psychiatry* (1957), part 3: http://www.youtube.com/watch?v=uYzYVr8xCTs&feature=relmfu (accessed March 27, 2016).

57. Tompkins et al., "Epilogue," 103.

58. Ibid., 101.

59. See, for instance, Bronislaw Malinowski, "Magic, Science, and Religion" (1925), in *Magic, Science, Religion, and Other Essays* (1948; New York: Doubleday, 1954), 17–92; Max Weber, *The Sociology of Religion*, trans. Ephraim Fischoff (1922; Boston: Beacon Press, 1963); and Alfred Jules Ayer, *Language, Truth, and Logic* (New York: Oxford University Press, 1936), 115.

60. Gordon W. Allport, "Religion and Adolescence," in Klineberg et al., *Religion in the Developing Personality*, 2:33.

61. Allport, *The Individual and His Religion*, 68, 73, 139.

62. Ibid., 78, 73.

63. Ibid., 68.

64. Allport, "Religion and Adolescence."

65. Allport, "Behavioral Science, Religion, and Mental Health," 195.

66. Allport, *The Individual and His Religion*, 24; Allport, "Behavioral Science, Religion, and Mental Health," 193; Allport, *The Individual and His Religion*, 24. See also Paul Tillich, *Dynamics of Faith* (1957; New York: HarperOne, 2009); and, more recently, Alan Wolfe, *The Transformation of American Religion: How We Actually Live Our Faith* (New York: Free Press, 2003), 245–47.

67. Allport, *The Individual and His Religion*, 25.

68. Allport, "Behavioral Science, Religion, and Mental Health," 192, 189.

69. See Koenig, McCullough, and Larson, *Handbook of Religion and Health*, 214–19.

70. Allport, "Religion and Prejudice," 424, 422.

71. Ibid., 420–22.

Coda

1. A. Roy Eckardt, "The New Look in American Piety," *Christian Century* 17 (November 17, 1954), 1396.

2. See, for instance, William G. McLoughlin, *Revivals, Awakenings, and Reform* (Chicago: University of Chicago Press, 1978); and Jon Butler, *Awash in a Sea of Faith: Christianizing the American People* (Cambridge, Mass.: Harvard University Press, 1990).

3. Dwight D. Eisenhower, as quoted in William Lee Miller, *Piety along*

the *Potomac: Notes on Politics and Morals in the '50s* (Boston: Houghton Mifflin, 1964), 45–46.

4. Norman Vincent Peale, as quoted in "Enthusiasm Need for Conquest of Christian World," *Syracuse Post-Standard,* July 2, 1928.

5. American Foundation of Religion and Psychiatry, Confidential minutes of Administrative Meeting, November 27, 1960, Institutes of Religion and Health Records, Special Collections Research Center, Syracuse University Libraries (hereafter "IRH papers").

6. Elmer Hess, M.D., president of American Medical Association, and Norman Vincent Peale, *Medicine's Proclamation of Faith* (Atlantic City, N.J., June 7, 1955), 17; and "religiously motivated ideas": "Research—1. In Religion and Psychiatry," document attached to a letter from John M. Cotton to Dr. Bernard Barber, February 13, 1959; both publication and document are in IRH papers. On platforms see Samuel Z. Klausner, "The Religio-Psychiatric Movement: Changing Ideology of the Movement (Lecture II)," *Review of Religious Research* 6.1 (1964), 22.

7. Ira Katznelson, *Fear Itself: The New Deal and the Origins of Our Time* (New York: Liveright, 2013), 13, emphasis in original; Jonathan P. Herzog, *The Spiritual-Industrial Complex: America's Religious Battle against Communism in the Early Cold War* (New York: Oxford University Press, 2011).

8. Norman Vincent Peale to Edward F. Hutton, July 21, 1947, Norman Vincent Peale Papers, Special Collections Research Center, Syracuse University Libraries (hereafter "NVP papers").

9. Joel Osteen, *You Can, You Will: 8 Undeniable Qualities of a Winner* (New York: FaithWords-Hachette, 2014), 11; David Van Biema and Jeff Chu, "Does God Want You to Be Rich?" *Time,* September 18, 2006, 50.

10. Osteen, *You Can, You Will,* 10, 79, 82, 81; See also Barbara Ehrenreich, *Bright-Sided: How Positive Thinking Is Undermining America* (New York: Picador, 2009), 125–33; and Chris Lehmann, "Pentecostalism for the Exurbs: Joel Osteen's God Really Wants You to Dress Well, Stand Up Straight, and Get a Convenient Parking Space," *Slate,* January 2, 2008, http://www.slate.com/id/2180590.

11. Ted J. Kaptchuk and Franklin G. Miller, "Placebo Effects in Medicine," *New England Journal of Medicine* 373.8–9 (July 2015), doi:10.1056/NEJMp1504023. See also Susan Huculak, "The Placebo Effect in Psychiatry: Problem or Solution?" *Journal of Medical Ethics* 40 (2014), 376–80, doi: 10.1136/medethics-2013–101410; and Azgad Gold and Pesach Lichtenberg, "The Moral Case for the Clinical Placebo," *Journal of Medical Ethics* 40 (2014), 219–24, doi:10.1136/medethics-2012–101314.

12. Osteen, *You Can, You Will*, 94, 82.

13. Smiley Blanton, "Analytical Study of a Cure at Lourdes," *Psychoanalytic Quarterly* 9 (1940), 353.

14. Daniel C. Dennett, *Breaking the Spell: Religion as a Natural Phenomenon* (New York: Penguin, 2006), 178, emphasis in original.

15. Ibid., 204–5, emphasis in original.

16. Rodney Stark and Roger Finke, *Acts of Faith: Explaining the Human Side of Religion* (Berkeley: University of California Press, 2000), as quoted in Dennett, *Breaking the Spell*, 69, emphasis in original.

17. Dennett, *Breaking the Spell*, 177.

18. Ibid., 272.

19. Ibid., 276. The study mentioned is Jeffrey A. Dusek et al., "Study of the Therapeutic Effects of Intercessory Prayer (STEP): Study Design and Research Methods," *American Heart Journal* 143.4 (2002), 577–84. A follow-up study by Herbert Benson, J. Dusek, and J. Sherwood appears as "Study of the Therapeutic Effects of Intercessory Prayer (STEP) in Cardiac Bypass Patients: A Multicenter Randomized Trial of Uncertainty and Certainty of Receiving Intercessory Prayer," *American Heart Journal* 151.4 (April 2006), 934–42.

20. See Harold G. Koenig, Michael E. McCullough, and Donald B. Larson, *Handbook of Religion and Health*, 2nd edition (Oxford: Oxford University Press, 2012), especially 214–19.

21. Dennett, *Breaking the Spell*, 134, 334.

22. Sam Harris, *The End of Faith: Religion, Terror, and the Future of Reason* (New York: Norton, 2004), 72; and Harris, "God's Dupes," *Los Angeles Times*, March 15, 2007.

23. Richard Dawkins, *The God Delusion* (Boston: Houghton Mifflin, 2006), 308; also Dawkins, "How Dare You Call Me a Fundamentalist: The Right to Criticise 'Faith-Heads,'" *Times* (London), May, 12, 2007.

24. E. O. Wilson, *Consilience: The Unity of Knowledge* (New York: Knopf, 1998); Stephen Jay Gould, *Rocks of Ages: Science and Religion in the Fullness of Life* (New York: Ballantine, 1999), 5, based on his argument that science and religion represent "non-overlapping magisteria," in the essay carrying that title in *Natural History* 106.2 (1997), 16–22.

25. Gordon W. Allport, "Religion and Prejudice," chapter 28 of *The Nature of Prejudice* (New York: Anchor, 1954).

26. Gordon W. Allport, *The Individual and His Religion: A Psychological Interpretation* (New York: Macmillan, 1950), 64–65.

27. Rev. Noël Mailloux, as quoted in Academy of Religion and Mental Health, *Religion, Science, and Mental Health: Proceedings of the First Academy*

Symposium on Inter-discipline Responsibility for Mental Health—A Religious and Scientific Concern, 1957 (New York: New York University Press, 1959), 65.

28. David Ray Griffin, *Religion and Scientific Naturalism: Overcoming the Conflicts* (Albany, N.Y.: SUNY Press, 2000), 12.

29. See, for instance, Asa Gray, *Darwiniana: Essays and Reviews Pertaining to Darwinism* (New York: D. Appleton, 1876); also James R. Moore, *The Post-Darwinian Controversies: A Study of the Protestant Struggle to Come to Terms with Darwin in Great Britain and America, 1870–1900* (Cambridge: Cambridge University Press, 1979).

30. Dennett, *Breaking the Spell*, 220. Regarding psychiatric diagnosis, see "Histrionic Personality Disorder," in American Psychiatric Association, *Diagnostic and Statistical Manual of Mental Disorders: DSM-5*, 5th edition (Washington, D.C.: APA, 2013), 301.50, where it is still formally identified by markers such as "self-dramatization," being "suggestible," and conveying a "shifting and shallow expression of emotions."

31. Harris, *Waking Up: A Guide to Spirituality without Religion* (New York: Simon and Schuster, 2014), especially 11–33.

32. To invoke a well-known example, founding father and theist Thomas Jefferson, while serving in office, removed from his Bible the many parts that he considered supernatural, false, or distractingly magical. Gone were the Virgin Birth, the miracles, and the Resurrection. He called the amended text, completed in 1820, *The Life and Morals of Jesus of Nazareth, Extracted Textually from the Gospels in Greek, Latin, French, and English.*

33. Kenneth T. Walsh with Jeff Kass, "Separate Worlds," *U.S. News and World Report*, October 17, 2004.

34. Robert D. Putnam and David E. Campbell, *American Grace: How Religion Divides and Unites Us* (New York: Simon and Schuster, 2010), 9.

35. Ibid., 10.

36. Ibid., 16–17. See also John S. Dickerson, "The Decline of Evangelical America," *New York Times*, December 15, 2012; and Adam Lee, "Godless Millennials Could End the Political Power of the Religious Right," *Guardian*, October 26, 2014, both of which draw on a wide range of studies and data.

37. Lee, "Godless Millennials," citing the Pew Research Center's Religion and Public Life Project, "'Nones' on the Rise," October 9, 2012, http://www.pewforum.org/2012/10/09/nones-on-the-rise/; and "What Is Your Religion ... If Any?" *USA Today*, http://usatoday30.usatoday.com/graphics/news/gra/gnoreligion/flash.htm (accessed March 27, 2016), citing the 2001 American Religious Identification Survey by the Graduate Center of the City University of New York, http://www.gc.cuny.edu/CUNY_GC/media/CUNY-Graduate-Center/PDF/ARIS/ARIS-PDF-version.pdf.

38. Lee, "Godless Millennials," citing the Pew Research Center's American Values Survey Question Database, http://www.people-press.org/values-questions/q41d/i-never-doubt-the-existence-of-god/#generation.

39. "U.S. Christians numbers 'Decline Sharply,' Poll Finds," *BBC News Online*, May 12, 2015, http://www.bbc.com/news/world-us-canada-32710444. See also Mark A. Smith, *Secular Faith: How Culture Has Trumped Religion in American Politics* (Chicago: University of Chicago Press, 2015).

40. Putnam and Campbell, *American Grace*, 120.

Acknowledgments

Much of this book was written during a sabbatical leave from Northwestern University, and I thank the Dean's Office of Weinberg College of Arts and Sciences for making that extended time available. For wonderful support over the years I owe a big debt of thanks to friends and neighbors in Peru, among whom this book was written and extensively discussed. In particular, Mariella Mazzei Bedregal, Mauricio Lavarello, and Catty Velasquez—respectively, a journalist and owners of a small printing company—expected regular progress reports, naturally in Spanish, which kept me on a tight and focused schedule while doing wonders for my fluency. From Northwestern, Alex Ruiz and Carlos Hurtado helped keep my online library accessible. Maha Jafri, my superb research assistant, scanned much-needed documents in Evanston at crucial intervals. Victoria Zahrobsky at the Interlibrary Loan Office processed a small stream of complex requests with patience and humor.

The Special Collections Research Center staff at Syracuse

University Libraries went to great lengths to locate the many documents cited here. Nicole Dittrich, Nicolette Dobrowolski, and William La Moy, in particular, were an extraordinary help on several occasions and tireless in their search for letters and memos that had been misfiled. I am grateful for permission to quote from documents and reproduce photographs and other materials found in the Institutes of Religion and Health Records Special Collection and the Norman Vincent Peale Papers Special Collection. I am grateful also to George Hart at the Peale History Center and Library in Pawling, New York, for granting me access to the large Peale archive at the Syracuse University Libraries, sharing photographs, and allowing me to reproduce and quote from a sizable number of controversial documents.

In New York City, senior administrators at what is now the Blanton-Peale Institute and Counseling Center met with me graciously one humid summer afternoon. Special thanks to Nunzio Gubitosa, Jane Roberts, and Nancy Moore Simpson, leaders at an institute that has changed beyond recognition since the decades described here.

Laurie Shannon, my department chair, and Susan Manning, my interim chair, supported this book in numerous ways. I am grateful as well to the remarkable staff that keeps Northwestern English running daily: Nathan Mead, Dave Kuzel, Jennifer Britton, and the incomparable Kathy Daniels, all of whom have helped me greatly in preparing my text and images for production. Warm thanks also to my colleagues in the department, in particular Nick Davis, Christine Froula, Reg Gibbons, Chris Herbert, Jules Law, Carl Smith, and Julia Stern, and, in Northwestern History, to Ken Alder, Deborah Cohen, Laura Hein, and Mike Sherry.

I am profoundly grateful to the external readers whom

Yale University Press asked to evaluate the manuscript. Their detailed, incisive reports were invaluable in guiding me through the revisions and drawing out my central argument. My debt to Kevin Kruse is considerable, not least for the research he completed in *One Nation under God,* fortunately (for me) without exhaustive focus on Peale. Special thanks as well to Jennifer Banks, my editor at Yale, who helped in countless additional ways to sharpen and improve this book.

Vivian Wheeler and Mary Pasti, my copyeditors, deserve warm and profuse thanks for their meticulous attention to the manuscript. Wendy Strothman and Lauren MacLeod at the Strothman Agency provided support and assistance at just the right moments. Thanks also to Heather Gold at Yale for guiding the preparation of the book for production.

Friends in Chicago and family in England cheered the project on and sustained me through the many hours of research and revision. I am especially grateful to Alyson Carter, Carol Donnelly, Ed Hirschland, and Chris Lonn. Chief and special thanks go to Jorge Arce, who once again lived with me through all of it, and to the Arce family, in both Chicago and Peru, for their love, laughter, and extraordinary support.

Index

Academy of Religion and Mental
Health, 123–36, 142–45,
153–54; ecumenicalism of, 136;
"Religion, Science and Mental
Health" (1957 symposium),
128, 134–35, 137–40; against
secularism, 137–38; and "soul
sickness," 132; against zealotry,
137, 153
Adler, Alfred, and "inferiority
feelings," 76
Advertising Council: "Religion in
American Life" campaign, 69
Affluence, 109; as spiritual
"reward," 85
AFRAP. *See* American Founda-
tion of Religion and Psychiatry,
Inc.
Agnosticism, 136, 156
Alcoholism, 44
Allport, Gordon W. (psychologist),
126–27, 141–45, 154; and
"immature" belief, 133; and
"mature" belief, 132–33; on

religion and race prejudice, 133,
144–45
American Foundation of Religion
and Psychiatry, Inc. (Peale,
president), 6, 12–17, 20–29,
35–36, 42, 44, 55, 71, 79, 86–88,
94, 96, 101–9, 121–23, 132–36,
142, 147, 154; as global initiative, 23–24, 123, 129; interracial,
23; and mass counseling, 88, 94,
113; nonsectarian, 30; proselytizing, 23, 30, 36, 56, 87–88,
121, 132, 135; services to
corporations, 108, 113; and
"spiritual healing," 112–13,
115–17, 122, 136; support for
pharmaceuticals, 110
Americanism, 63–64, 72, 96, 99,
154; Peale's crusade for, 148. *See
also* Nationalism; Patriotism
American Legion: "Back to God"
crusade, 10, 97
American Medical Association,
107, 120–21